What a Character!

AMERICAN WAR HEROES

Notable Lives in History

Marilyn Boyer

First printing: September 2023

Master Books, P.O. Box 726, Green Forest, AR 72638

Master Books® is a division of the New Leaf Publishing Group, LLC.

ISBN: 978-1-68344-342-1
ISBN: 978-1-61458-868-9 (digital)
Library of Congress Control Number: 2023942257

Cover: Diana Bogardus
Interior: Terry White

Please consider requesting that a copy of this volume be purchased by your local library system.

Printed in the United States of America

Please visit our website for other great titles:
www.masterbooks.com

For information regarding promotional opportunities, please contact the publicity department at pr@nlpg.com.

Master Books®
A Division of New Leaf Publishing Group
www.masterbooks.com

Table of Contents

Images are AI-generated at shutterstock.com

Maps:

Map Trek: Atlas of the World & U.S. History – pages 38, 58, 68, 80, 92, 104

shutterstock.com – page 110

The American War of Independence

Officially, the War of Independence, often called the American Revolution, began on July 4, 1776, when the Continental Congress adopted the Declaration of Independence. However, the bloodshed had begun the previous year on April 19 with the battles of Lexington and Concord.

Tensions had been rising between the thirteen English colonies in North America and the mother country for many years. Colonists accused King George and Parliament of having violated their rights as English subjects. Although modern history texts rank taxation without representation in Parliament as the cause of the war, in fact the Declaration lists twenty-seven reasons the colonies were choosing to separate from the British Empire and form a new nation. Among these other reasons were the Crown's interference with American courts and local governments, inciting the Indian tribes to fight against the colonists, and the quartering of British troops in private homes against the wishes of the owners. Finally, enough colonists believed that their rights were safe only under a new government, and Congress had voted for independence.

The British march from Boston on the morning of April 19, 1776, had two purposes. The first was to arrest colonial leaders John Hancock and Samuel Adams who were staying at a private home in Lexington. The second purpose was to advance to nearby Concord where arms, ammunition, and supplies were believed to be stored for the purpose of opposing the British regulars with force if it became necessary. However, American spies had learned of the plan and messengers had ridden through the night of the 18th to give warning to the patriots. Adams and Hancock fled well ahead of the king's troops and colonists streamed to Concord to move the supplies and stop the Redcoats. After a fight at Concord, the British were driven back to Boston and besieged there. Even after this early bloodshed, the colonies sent petitions to the king and Parliament asking for peace and a restoration of their rights. However, diplomacy failed and the king's next actions — including the hiring of mercenaries from other nations — to bring the colonies back under control, made it clear to Congress that independence was the only way to preserve American rights.

After seven years of war, the colonies won their independence and soon had established a new nation. In 1789, the Constitution was ratified and the United States of America was born.

1

Ethan Allen and His Green Mountain Boys

| May 10, 1775 | During the battles at Lexington and Concord |

The news of the battle at Lexington and Concord in Massachusetts had spread across the colonies rapidly. There had been trouble between the king of England and his American colonists for many years, so the news did not surprise many people on the farms and in the towns of New England. Few were as prepared for war as Ethan Allen and the Green Mountain Boys.

Trouble Brewing

Ethan Allen was a farmer. Born in the Connecticut colony in 1738, he had become a leader in what is now Vermont after moving there and establishing his farm. There was conflict in those days because both New York and New Hampshire claimed the right to sell the land to settlers. The men from Connecticut had bought their farms from New Hampshire. When the government of New York told them they had to pay the New York colonial government for the land as well, trouble was sure to follow.

Allen organized his neighbors into a **militia**. They called themselves the Green Mountain Boys. When New York sent a sheriff or other official to make the settlers pay a second time for their land, Ethan and the Boys sent them packing. It was the trouble with New York that had caused the Green Mountain Boys to organize in the first place, and it was part of their training for the war with England that would soon follow.

> **militia:** A military force raised from the civil population to be called up on short notice

They were not well-trained like the British soldiers. They did not look much like soldiers. They had no uniforms, so every man wore whatever clothing he had. When they gathered for a meeting or a fight, they looked like most other frontiersmen of their time. **Lindsey-woolsey** shirts, **buckskin** moccasins, fringed buckskin hunting coats, and homespun breeches were common. They wore all sorts of hats, made at home by mothers, sisters, and wives. These might be in any shape and made from the skins of beaver, squirrel, raccoon, or bear.

They did not have regular army equipment, either. There was not a **bayonet** on any gun they carried. But for the type of fighting that would take place when the war reached their mountains, the Green Mountain Boys were very fit. Though they lacked bayonets, their guns were still deadly.

Lindsey-woolsey: A strong coarse fabric of linen and wool

buckskin: Made from the skin of a male deer

bayonet: A blade fixed to the muzzle of a gun

While the British army still used smooth-bore muskets, the frontiersmen mostly carried rifles. Muskets were not accurate. They could only be used at close range. That was one reason why the British soldiers relied on their bayonets so much. The rifles of the Green Mountain militiamen, however, had grooved, or "rifled" barrels. They were much more accurate than muskets and the frontiersmen had depended on them to shoot game for themselves. The hard-working families in their rough log homes needed the meat from the forest to survive. These men had become experts at hitting a target even a hundred yards away. They would soon prove to be deadly enemies to British regulars in the bright red coats which made such easy targets in the woods.

Ethan Allen was proud of his men, and he was just the sort of leader they needed. He was a big, tough man. He stood well over six feet tall, much taller than the average American at that time. It was said that he was so strong he could pick up a 100-pound sack of salt with his teeth and sling it up onto his back. He knew how to influence people, and his men were glad to follow him and were very loyal. He also knew how to talk to his enemies. He could **bluff** and threaten with the best of them when that was what was needed. When news of the war against England came, the men and their leader were ready.

bluff: Trick

When the story of Lexington and Concord came to the Green Mountains, Allen immediately called his men to assemble. He later said, "The first systematical and bloody attempt at Lexington to enslave America thoroughly electrified my mind, and fully determined me to take part with my country."[1] The Boys were quick to answer the call. Buckskin-clad men left their hayfields, picked up their long rifles, and headed for the meeting place. Less than a month after the Battle of Lexington, the militia was ready for a fight.

Fort Ticonderoga (ti-con-dero-ga)

Allen set his sights on Fort Ticonderoga on Lake Champlain. In those days, armies often had to travel and move supplies by water, and the waterways of Champlain, the Hudson River, and Lake George could all be controlled by the guns of Fort Ticonderoga. Since the British held

　　　　　　　　　　　　　　　　　America's War Heroes

Canada, this fort could prevent an attack from that direction. First, the fort had to be taken from the British.

Ticonderoga had been a French fort until the end of the French and Indian War. When the British took over there, they had not kept the fort in good repair. Its position still made it a barrier to any ship attempting to sail past. Every patriot in New England understood that Ticonderoga needed to be conquered early in the war. In Allen's home colony of Connecticut, some leading patriots took action to help. They persuaded the colony's leaders to take 300 **pounds** from the treasury for the task. It was sent to Ethan Allen to buy powder and bullets and to pay his men.

pounds: British money

Allen was moving ahead with his preparations, acting with the energy that people had learned to expect from him. He had first gathered all the Green Mountain Boys in the area of Bennington. Then a rider was sent to bring down other Boys from the north. He wanted a large force in place for the attack on Ticonderoga, which he had decided to launch on May 10. The Boys were to gather on the shore of Lake Champlain at a place called Hand's Cove.

The militia leader had sent a spy into the fort to report on conditions inside. The man persuaded the British soldiers to let him in by saying that he needed the services of the fort's barber. His bushy beard had grown too long in his wilderness travels, and he wanted a shave. He got one, and along with it, he got some useful information from the barber, who seemed to enjoy chatting with his customers.

During the shave, he learned that the post was held by only 50 British troops. That was enough to keep the barber busy, but not enough to keep such a large fort secure. He also found out that the fort was in a very bad condition.

The report was encouraging, but Allen knew that 50 British soldiers could hold the fort against a larger force outside. They had the advantage of the fort walls and many cannons. The attack on Ticonderoga would need the element of surprise.

All through the moonlit night of May 9, 1775, the Green Mountain Boys drifted into Hand's Cove. One by one or in small groups, they appeared from the woods with their deadly long rifles and as much food as they could carry. Ethan Allen was waiting for them with plenty of gunpowder and lead bullets. They stood chatting in the shadows of the trees, leaning on their rifles and waiting for orders from their leader.

Shortly after midnight there came the sound of galloping hooves and a rider appeared in the camp. The young officer was wearing a Connecticut uniform and he demanded to see Ethan Allen. He was taken to the campfire where Allen was talking with some of his leading men. The stranger announced that the Committee of Safety in Cambridge, Massachusetts, had placed him in command of this expedition. He waved a paper which he called his **commission**. He demanded that Allen turn over command to him.

commission: A formal document issued to appoint a named person to high office

The man's name was Benedict Arnold and he would someday become America's most famous **traitor**. However, that was far in the future. In the meantime, he would become an officer in the Continental Army and would fight bravely in several battles before going over to the enemy.

The mountain men standing around the campfire only knew that they were loyal to their leader, Ethan Allen, and they did not like the newcomer's attitude. They had volunteered to fight under Allen, and they declared that they would fight for him or not fight at all. Looking around at the grim, weathered faces of these pioneers, Arnold lost some of his confidence. When Allen offered to share command with him, Arnold accepted. No one doubted that Ethan Allen was in charge.

traitor: One who betrays his country

It was still dark when Allen packed 85 of his men into two boats and began the crossing of Lake Champlain to Ticonderoga. He had 200 men ready and eager to fight, but most would have to stay behind. There were only two boats, and the sky would be growing light before they could return for more soldiers. Surprise was the key to success.

Allen stood in the bow of the first boat, sword in hand. Behind him was Benedict Arnold. The rest of the boat was crowded with men talking in low tones as the muffled oars propelled them along to their appointment with history. After a mile of rowing, the dark walls of the fort appeared above them through the mist. Allen gathered his men on the shore and made a brief talk.

With Allen and Arnold leading the way, the Boys began climbing the hill toward the fort. Little was heard besides the quiet shuffling of feet and the wild cry of a **loon** in the distance. In the eastern sky, the first faint glow of dawn could be seen. Men were almost holding their breath. Would the surprise work? The wicket gate was just ahead; they would soon know.

> **loon:** A large black and white bird with red eyes

The Capture

Through the gloom, Allen made out the form of a sentry, lying on a bench beside the gate. Rasping snores told him that the man was asleep. Then someone stepped on a twig and suddenly the sentry, with a gasp, leaped up and threw his musket to his shoulder. Allen leaped forward, attempting to knock the barrel of the gun aside with his sword. But the musket misfired! Only the powder in the pan flashed, lighting up the faces of the sentry and several Green Mountain Boys.

For just an instant they were all blinded by the flash, then they were running, shouting after the sentry. The man was yelling a warning to the fort, but it was too late. Before the sleeping **Britishers** could rouse themselves and come pouring out of the barracks, the Boys were at the door. One redcoat leaped out and tried to stab one of the attackers with his bayonet, but Allen knocked the Britisher down with the flat of his sword. The man begged Allen not to kill him. He would live, Allen told him, if he would lead the Green Mountain Boys to the fort commander's door.

> **Britishers:** Native inhabitants of Great Britain

The frightened man led them up a flight of stairs in another building. Pounding on the door, Allen demanded, "Come out of there!" A British officer opened the door. Ethan Allen demanded that he surrender the fort immediately.

"By whose authority do you enter this fort?" the officer demanded.

In reply, Allen roared, "In the name of the great Jehovah and the Continental Congress!"[2]

He demanded an immediate and complete surrender. He claimed the fort and everything that belonged to it. If the demand was not granted, he said, not a man would be left alive. The captain surrendered his sword.

The other Green Mountain Boys had been busy **routing** the redcoats out of their beds, and they now stood in their nightclothes on the parade ground, unarmed. The fort had been taken without a shot being fired. After all their guns were collected, the men were returned to their barracks under guard.

> **routing:**
> Defeating and causing to retreat in disorder

The fort had become American property in only about an hour. The mountain men were a wild and rowdy lot, shouting and firing off their guns in celebration. The fort's cannons and provisions would be a great gift for Washington's new army. Riders were quickly sent out to spread the news. Soon the whole country was celebrating the victory.

The money from Connecticut had been well spent. Allen wrote to Governor Trumbull, telling him he was making him a present of a major, a captain, and two lieutenants in the regular establishment of George the Third. He had hopes they would serve as a **ransom** for

some of their captive friends held in Boston.

The fort's flag was sent to Congress in Philadelphia. It was in their name and the name of the Great Jehovah that it had been captured by Ethan Allen and the Green Mountain Boys.

2

Daniel Morgan and His Sharpshooters

1775–1781	The Battle of Cowpens During the Revolutionary War

Morgan's Early Years

Daniel Morgan, while fighting with the colonists and the British in the French and Indian War, distinguished himself as a fearless fighter and able leader of men. He came very close to dying when shot through the back of his neck in battle. The bullet went through his mouth and came out, knocking out all his teeth on the left side. He hovered between life and death for months, but finally recovered.

At the end of the French and Indian War, he returned home to his farm in Virginia. Soon after returning, he met and married Abigail Bailey, a loving Christian woman who inspired and encouraged him to change his rough ways and try to live a life that demonstrated that he was now a Christian man. She taught her husband to trust in God and become a man with an active prayer life.

Morgan recounts that just before the final attack of the fort at Quebec near the start of the Revolutionary War, he knelt in the cold, drifting snow and pled with God for the courage and strength to fight. His own soldiers attested to how after the victory at the Battle of Cowpens, which we shall explain later, they recalled him stopping his horse to pray aloud and with tears streaming down his face, thanking God for the victory.

His soldiers also said his men never **scoffed** at their leader's prayers, because they noticed that the harder "Old Dan Morgan," as they lovingly called him,

scoffed: mocked

prayed, the more certain they were that they were about to be engaged in a fearsome battle and they therefore welcomed his prayers to God.

Dan Morgan nor his wife had much formal schooling as children, but they **endeavored** to make up for lost time by **procuring** books and studying both early and late each day. Dan and his wife had two little girls and enjoyed building a Christ-centered atmosphere in their little home.

endeavored: To try hard to achieve something

About nine years later, a storm began to brew in the colonies for a war of independence from the British. Morgan watched carefully, and after the Battles of Lexington and Concord, the Continental Congress called for ten companies of soldiers from Pennsylvania, Maryland, and Virginia. Dan Morgan received a commission as captain five days after the Battle of Bunker Hill, which took place in Boston.

procuring: Acquiring

In less than ten days, Morgan, at the head of 96 expert **riflemen** from Virginia, set out for Boston. They marched the 600 miles in only 21 days without the loss of a single man.

rifleman: An infantry soldier armed with a long-rifled gun

Expedition to Quebec

Late in the fall of 1775, Morgan and his men, a band of **sharpshooters**, marched with about a thousand other troops, joining up with Benedict Arnold's ill-fated expedition to Quebec, Canada. In the attack on Quebec, Arnold was wounded and carried off the battlefield, and

sharpshooters: Elite corps of riflemen who provided precision shooting

General Montgomery, who was also leading the attack, was killed in action. Morgan took Arnold's place and fought like a hero. He forced his way into the city so far that he and all his men were surrounded, captured, and put into prison.

A British officer, on seeing Morgan's charge, greatly admired his courage and visited him in prison, offering him the rank and pay of colonel in the British army. Morgan quickly answered, "I hope, sir, you will never again insult me in my present distressed and unfortunate situation, by making me offers which plainly imply that you think me a **scoundrel**."[3]

scoundrel: A dishonest person

regiment: A military unit consisting of up to 10 companies

harass: To make small scale attacks on the enemy

outposts: A detachment of troops stationed at a distance from a main force to guard against surprise attacks

Congress voted Morgan a colonel's commission with orders to raise a **regiment** shortly after he was released from prison on a prisoner exchange. That regiment reported for duty in Morristown, New Jersey, during the long, hard winter of 1776. Five hundred of the best riflemen were chosen from various regiments to be under Colonel Morgan's command. Morgan's men, as they were known, were to always be at the front, watching every movement of the enemy, furnishing prompt and accurate information about the enemy to General Washington. Part of their job was to **harass** the British, fighting with the enemy's **outposts** for every inch of ground.

British General Burgoyne, meanwhile, in the fall of 1777, marched down from Canada with a large group of British, **Hessians**, and Native Americans through the Hudson Valley. Although Washington could hardly spare Morgan's men, he felt compelled to help drive back the invaders, so sent Morgan's men on that mission.

There were two great battles that helped to seal Burgoyne's fate — the Battle of Freeman's Farm and the Battle of Saratoga. The British officers, clad in their bright red uniforms, were easy targets for Morgan's sharpshooters. Morgan's men became a terror to the Hessians. As Morgan proclaimed, "The very sight of my riflemen was always enough for the Hessian **pickets**. They would scamper into their lines as if the devil drove them, shouting in all the English they knew, 'Rebel in da bush! Rebel in da bush!'"[4]

Hessians: German troops hired by the British to help fight against the Americans

pickets: Soldiers posted on guard ahead of the main force

When Burgoyne eventually surrendered, he took Morgan warmly by the hand and said, "Sir, you command the finest regiment in the world."[5] For the next year and a half, after the victory at Saratoga, Morgan and his men were engaged in **incessant** attacks on the enemy's outposts. Just prior to the Battle of Monmouth, Morgan had an attack of **sciatica**, brought on by constant exposure to the weather and hardships, which forced him to leave the army for a while.

incessant: Something repeated without pause

sciatica: Pain affecting the back, hip, and outside of the leg

After General Gate was defeated at Camden, however, Morgan declared that no man should have any regard for himself when his country was in peril. He hurried down south and took his old position as colonel. After his performance at the Battle of King's Mountain, Congress made Morgan a **brigadier general**.

brigadier general: An officer of the army, who holds a rank junior to a major general but senior to a colonel, usually commanding a brigade

upland: Hilly ground above sea level

garrisons: Permanent military installations

wagoner: A person who drove a wagonload of supplies across the mountains

The Battle of Cowpens

The Battle of Cowpens, however, became his glorious victory, one in which he was able to plan as well as fight. It's been said that as to the tactics used, this was perhaps the most brilliant battle of the war for independence.

Cowpens was in **upland** South Carolina and so named as it was a pasture where local farmers penned their cattle. General Nathaniel Greene, in an effort to cut Cornwallis off from the seacoast, gave Morgan command of one thousand men, with orders to march to the southwest and threaten inland posts and their **garrisons**.

Cornwallis, the English earl, hardly knew which way to turn, but decided to follow Greene's example by dividing his army as well. He sent Colonel Banastre Tarleton, known for his cruelty in battle, to crush Morgan. Tarleton was confident he could do so and set up to pounce upon "the old **wagoner**" and crush him with a single blow.

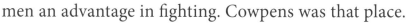

Tarleton called Morgan this because one of Morgan's jobs in the French and Indian War had been wagoner for the British army.

Morgan skillfully began to fall back until he found a place that was well-suited and would give his men an advantage in fighting. Cowpens was that place. A broad, deep river lay in the rear and would serve to cut off all hope of retreat. Morgan said he chose this so that his men would know they had no option to run away, but must fight or die.

The patriot army at Cowpens encamped the night before the expected battle, but a trusty American acting as a spy was sent to Tarleton to say that the Americans had **faced about**, waiting to fight sometime the next day. That night Morgan went around the many campfires of his men encouraging them with comforting, fatherly words. "Stand by me, boys, and the old wagoner will crack his whip for sure over Tarleton tomorrow."[6]

faced about: To turn and face in the opposite direction

Tarleton, eager to get an early start, put his army in motion by three in the morning. However, that was not early enough to catch the old rifleman napping. Morgan rested his men at night, gave them a hearty breakfast early, and when Tarleton and his men showed up at sunrise, he found the patriots waiting and ready.

strategically: In a way that relates to a military advantage

skirmish line: A preliminary battle involving troops in front of the main force

Morgan **strategically** placed his riflemen in the **skirmish line**. These were men so skilled they could bring a squirrel down from the tallest tree. Colonel Pickens commanded the militia which was in place 300 yards in front of the hill. Along the **brow**, 150 yards behind the militia were **veterans** of the Continental line. Beyond the brow of the hill, Morgan stationed Colonel William Washington with his cavalry, out of sight and poised to move in an instant's notice.

Orders to the militia were to be firm: keep cool, take good aim, give two volleys at killing distance, and then fall back. Morgan encouraged the **Continentals** not to lose heart when the skirmishers and militia fell back. "Stand firm, and fire low. Listen for my turkey call."[7] Morgan often used a small turkey call that hunters would use to **decoy** turkeys. He would blow it in the heat of battle to tell the boys he was there, alive, and watching them fight.

Tarleton, **cocky** as ever, marched his men all night through the mud. They were exhausted and hungry. Tarleton, anxious to start the battle, informed his men that they could eat breakfast only after they crushed "the old wagoner."

When the battle began in earnest, the militia fired their well-aimed **volley**, and then fell back behind

brow: The top part of a hill or the edge of something high such as a cliff or rock

veterans: Men who had fighting experience

Continentals: Regular armed forces

decoy: Imitating a turkey call to lure a turkey toward the hunter's position

cocky: Arrogant

volley: When an attacking army lets loose a barrage of bullets all at once

the Continentals, who fell slightly back to save their **left flank**, when Tarleton sent his full force upon them. The veterans stood their ground and kept pouring on a heavy fire. Morgan then saw his **golden chance**.

> **left flank:** Side, generally a weaker spot

The shrill whistle of the turkey call rang out and Morgan's voice was heard to say, "Face about! One good fire and the victory is ours!"[8] Like a thunderbolt, Colonel William Washington's troops swept down in a semi-circle around the hill and charged the enemy's right flank. Instantly, the veterans faced about, opened up a deadly fire, and charged the confused British line with bayonets. It was over in just a few minutes. The old wagoner had set his trap and the British were caught.

> **golden chance:** An excellent chance to accomplish a goal

Six hundred British surrendered and threw down their guns, crying for **quarter**. The rest, including Tarleton himself, fled by horseback. In the Battle of Cowpens, the British lost 230, killed and wounded. The Americans had only 12 killed and 61 wounded.

> **quarter:** Mercy

Morgan, having just accomplished this amazing victory, did not rest yet, however. He knew Cornwallis and Tarleton would try to crush him again before he could manage to join up with General Nathaniel Greene's men. Morgan and his men got to the Catawba River two days ahead of the British and, with Greene's help, managed to cross it with all their men and **booty**.

> **booty:** Enemy equipment or property captured on the battlefield

Before his service to the army ended, Morgan took part in campaigns with Mad Anthony Wayne and Lafayette, which led to the capture of Cornwallis at Yorktown. Morgan had taken part in 50 battles and was elected to Congress twice and so served his country in both war and peace.

Alleghenies: The western part of the Appalachian Mountains; extending from northern Pennsylvania to southwestern Virginia

If you ever have the opportunity to visit Spartanburg, South Carolina, be sure to look for the figure of Daniel Morgan, under which is inscribed these words: "Daniel Morgan, the old Wagoner of the **Alleghenies** and Hero of Cowpens."

3

Francis Marion, the Swamp Fox

| 1775–1783 | During the Revolutionary War |

In 1780, the Revolutionary War was going badly for the Americans of South Carolina. Most of the American forces in the state had been defeated by the British and were captured or scattered. The main American army under General Moultrie had been conquered at the fall of Charleston, leaving only small bands of fighters called **partisans** to carry on the war in the south.

partisans: Strong supporters of the cause, fighting secretly

gamecock: Feather of a rooster bred and trained in game fighting

Andrew Pickens led a group of partisans who fought in the northeastern part of the state. Thomas Sumter was the leader of a band that opposed the British in the central part of South Carolina. He was known as the "Gamecock" because he was a bold fighter and wore a **gamecock** feather in his hat as a decoration.

The most famous of these partisan leaders was Francis Marion. He had been born and raised in South Carolina. As a boy, Marion had spent much of his time hunting and fishing in the swamps. He knew the Carolina wilderness as well as another boy might know his backyard. The dark forest and the marshes were his hunting grounds and he knew the hidden trails as well as the Native Americans did. Those days of **stalking** through the swamps taught him skills that would serve him well in the years to come. His sharp eyes

stalking: To pursue stealthily

could trace a faint path where the deer had traveled. He could hear and understand the forest sounds, following the gobble of a wild turkey or the whistle of a quail to find the best hunting. The

America's War Heroes

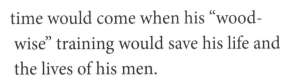

time would come when his "wood-wise" training would save his life and the lives of his men.

Francis Marion was born in 1732 on a plantation near Berkeley, South Carolina. He was the youngest child in a family of six children. His parents, Gabriel and Esther Marion, were **French Huguenots**. Their families had fled from France because they were persecuted for their religious beliefs. Like thousands of other colonists, they had come to America for religious freedom. Like most of their neighbors, they were farmers. South Carolina produced large crops of tobacco, rice, and **indigo**. From Charleston Harbor, ships took great loads of Carolina farm products to be sold in England.

> **French Huguenots:** French Protestants

> **indigo:** A tropical plant of the pea family, which was formerly widely cultivated as a source of dark blue dye

Cherokee War

Francis got his first taste of warfare when the Cherokees living near the Blue Ridge Mountains began attacking the settlers. The colonial government called for volunteers to fight the Cherokees. Francis Marion was now a young man and answered the call for soldiers.

Fighting the Cherokees taught him many important lessons about fighting. These fierce warriors were clever as well as brave. They were experts at fooling their enemies. They would hide in ambush and strike without warning. Then they would disappear back into the forests where they were very hard to find and attack.

Marion was respected by his neighbors for his courage and his honest character. They elected him to the First South Carolina Provincial Congress in 1775. War with England was coming, and his wisdom was needed in the government.

When the war began, he was elected captain of the Second South Carolina Regiment. Colonel Moultrie was their commander.

When the British navy tried to sail into Charleston Harbor in June of 1776 to capture Charleston, Moultrie and his men built a fort on nearby Sullivan's Island to stop them. The fort's defenses consisted of two log walls with sand packed in between. When the British cannonballs struck the walls, the flexible **palmetto** logs allowed the balls through but did not break. The cannonballs buried themselves in the sand between the walls and did no harm.

palmetto: A type of palm tree

Meanwhile, a detachment of British soldiers was to attack from the rear by marching from a nearby island. But they found that the channel between them and Sullivan's Island was too deep to wade across. The only bloodshed they experienced that day was in their battles with the swamp mosquitoes that descended on them in clouds. The Battle of Fort Moultrie ended poorly for the soldiers of the king.

Charleston

In 1780, the British came back to attack Charleston with a larger force. By then, Colonel Moultrie had been promoted to General and Francis Marion was a Lieutenant Colonel. Shortly before the British attacked, he was present at a party being held in Charleston. When Marion started to leave early in the evening, his friends stopped him. There was a silly custom then that no one should leave a party early. Someone stepped between him and the door as he tried to exit.

Marion was not a man who was easy to stop. Going quickly to a window, he leaped out. But the window was on the second story of the home and his ankle twisted under him as he hit the ground. He forced himself not to cry out as the pain shot up his leg. His ankle was broken! This was indeed a bad accident. He was an officer, and a battle was soon to begin.

He would miss the battle of Charleston. Moultrie ordered all officers who were not able to fight to leave the city. They could do no good for the army, and there was no sense in taking a chance on being captured by the British, so Marion's servant, Oscar, helped him mount his horse and together they rode home to Pond Bluff, Marion's plantation.

When Charleston fell, it appeared that the British now controlled both Georgia and South Carolina. British General Cornwallis expected now to be able to march his army north and join the other British forces fighting against George Washington's little patriot army. Francis Marion and some other brave Americans, fighting in small independent bands, would soon show that the fighting in the Carolinas was far from over.

Becoming the Swamp Fox

General Washington had sent General Horatio Gates to command what was left of the American army in the south. Now Gates sent out an order for all American officers who were still free to join him at Camden, South Carolina. Francis Marion gathered as many men as he could find who were willing to fight and led them north toward Camden. With him were his friend, Peter Horry (pronounced Or-ee), and Oscar, who had grown up with Francis and was his friend as well as his servant.

The little group did not look much like soldiers. There were about 20 men and boys, most of them dressed in **homespun** and riding their farm horses. Some of these men were white, some of them were black, and none of them had proper clothing and equipment for war. When they reached the army camp at Camden there were smiles and snickers at their appearance. But Colonel Marion sat tall in the saddle at the head of his men. He knew they would fight well when the time came.

homespun: Simple homemade clothes

General Gates was not impressed with the Marion band. He did not want such ragged-looking soldiers in his army. Someone did want Colonel Marion and his homespun fighters. A militia group had formed at Williamsburg to fight the British and their **Tory** comrades. General Gates sent Marion and his men to help them.

Tory: Colonists who supported Britain

The welcome they received at Williamsburg was different from the one they received from Gates. Shouts and cheers greeted them. These Carolinians wanted to fight. Marion had a reputation as a fighter, and they were happy to have him as their new leader.

Marion went right to work with his combined force. Up and down the Santee River they marched, burning or destroying every boat or raft that Cornwallis could use to ferry his soldiers across on his way to fight Washington. His men could see that they were now following a leader who intended to keep the British too busy in the Carolinas to go anywhere.

Then news came. Gates had been badly defeated at the Battle of Camden. Nearly a thousand Americans had been taken prisoner. Many more had been killed and wounded. Gates had fled to Charlotte, North Carolina. He had left his soldiers far behind. The army was shattered.

This left Marion and the other partisan leaders as the only forces to stand against the British in the south. It was not a small job. Thomas Sumter had been defeated at Fishing Creek by Colonel Banastre Tarleton, who was known for his cruelty to captured American soldiers. It would be a long time before he could gather a fighting force again. Many in the Carolinas were Tories, still loyal to the British king. The fighting would be tough and bloody.

The Man for the Job

Francis Marion was the man for the job. He was familiar with the swamps and used skills he had learned from the Cherokees to hide his camps and spy on enemy forces. Keeping his plans to himself, he led his men in attacks on unsuspecting British camps. They struck like lightning, often at night. Then they would scatter and escape through the dense forests and gather once again. They took with them captured supplies that were badly needed. They were always short of food and ammunition, so they took these whenever they could. They also needed fresh horses, so the British supplied these as well, though not voluntarily.

At Nelson's Ferry on the Santee River, they surprised a British force at dawn. The Tories and British soldiers were so surprised that they did not defend themselves well. While they were gathering their weapons, Marion's men thundered through the camp, shooting. Their wild cries terrified the men who had been awakened suddenly from sleep or surprised in the middle of building their breakfast campfires. The enemy scattered in panic, leaving the partisans to gather weapons, supplies, and horses. They also set free 150 Continental soldiers who had been captured at Camden. If any of these men had been among those who had laughed at Marion's soldiers earlier at Camden, they were not laughing now.

Colonel Tarleton chased Marion, hungry for revenge. But Marion moved from place to place often and was hard to find. His scouts and spies were everywhere, watching the movements of Tarleton and the Tories. Again and again, Marion's men surprised their enemies, but the British never could trap him.

Once Tarleton chased Marion for over 20 miles, only to lose the trail as the partisans scattered through the swamps. Finally, Tarleton gave up. Turning to his men, he angrily ordered them to turn around. "The devil himself couldn't catch that old swamp fox!" he snarled.[9] Marion's famous nickname was born.

On and on went the war. Cornwallis kept trying to move north, but Marion kept attacking the British and Tories so that they were always busy trying to catch him.

At Fort Mott, Marion's men forced the British to surrender by shooting flaming arrows to set the fort on fire. At Fort Watson, they built a tower of logs so they could shoot over the fort's walls. Always, he was outsmarting his enemies by using the lessons he had learned in the Cherokee war. His men were often hungry and poorly dressed. They had to make their own swords out of saw blades. They slept on the ground and drank swamp water. Some of them had to go home for a time and take care of their farms. However, they loved their leader and respected his fighting skill. He could always collect men for a battle when he needed them.

The amazing dedication of Marion and his men to the cause of freedom impressed even his enemies. One British officer, sent to meet with the Swamp Fox about exchanging prisoners, saw it firsthand. After he and Marion had arranged the exchange, he was invited to stay in the camp and share lunch before returning to his commander. When he saw that the meal was a mug of river water and a sweet potato roasted in the fire and served on a bark plate, the Britisher became curious.

"Is this your usual fare in this camp, Mr. Marion?" he asked.

"Indeed sir, and it is fortunate that we have more than usual today, as you have been so kind as to favor us with your company."

"Not an abundant allowance for which men would gladly risk their lives," the soldier muttered. "Are you and your men paid well for your service?"

"We are not paid at all, sir," Marion replied.

"Then — with all respect, sir — just why is it that you are opposing the might of the His Majesty's army?"

"Ah, I fight because I am in love, sir."

"In love?"

"Oh, yes! I am in love with a lady named Liberty, and for her I will gladly fight and die."[10]

The young British officer finished his meager meal and was blindfolded for the trip out of the swamp. He returned to his camp and gave his report about the arrangements made to trade American prisoners for British. Then he resigned his commission as a soldier.
Asked why he did so, he replied, "Sir, we are fighting men who are so consumed with their passion for independence that they are willing to live on roots and swamp water. No army will ever defeat them."[11]

Meanwhile, events were shaping up that were about to lead to an end to the war. General Washington had made the wise decision to send General Nathaniel Greene to replace Gates. Along with him came "Light Horse Harry" Lee, another brilliant officer. Daniel Morgan, the frontier militia commander, brought his buckskin-clad mountain men. After defeating the British and Tories at battles such as King's Mountain and Cowpens, the Americans fought their way east and bottled up the British forces in Charleston. News soon came that Washington had defeated Cornwallis at Yorktown. The war was over, so the British in Charleston were allowed to leave peacefully.

Francis Marion gathered his men for one final time. In a short speech, he praised them for their courage and loyalty. He told them how proud he was of them for their many great sacrifices during the war. Then, with a full heart, he turned his horse's head toward home.

His plantation, Pond Bluff, had suffered much damage during the war. Marion and his friend Oscar set to work and finally restored it to its former beauty. He married a fine lady and was very happy. Again, he was elected to the state senate, where a resolution was passed praising him for "his important services to this country." The Swamp Fox would never be forgotten.

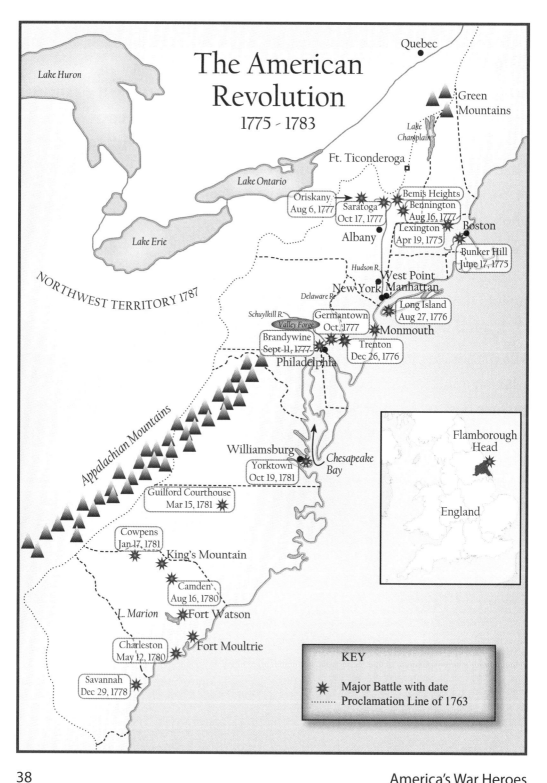

The American Revolution
1775 - 1783

Lake Huron

Quebec

Green Mountains

Lake Champlain

Ft. Ticonderoga

Lake Ontario

Oriskany
Aug 6, 1777

Saratoga
Oct 17, 1777

Bemis Heights

Bennington
Aug 16, 1777

Albany

Lexington
Apr 19, 1775

Boston

Lake Erie

NORTHWEST TERRITORY 1787

Hudson R.

West Point

Bunker Hill
June 17, 1775

Delaware R.

New York Manhattan

Schuylkill R.

Valley Forge

Germantown
Oct, 1777

Monmouth

Long Island
Aug 27, 1776

Brandywine
Sept 11, 1777

Trenton
Dec 26, 1776

Philadelphia

Appalachian Mountains

Williamsburg

Yorktown
Oct 19, 1781

Chesapeake Bay

Flamborough Head

Guilford Courthouse
Mar 15, 1781

England

Cowpens
Jan 17, 1781

King's Mountain

Camden
Aug 16, 1780

L. Marion

Fort Watson

Charleston
May 12, 1780

Fort Moultrie

KEY

Savannah
Dec 29, 1778

✴ Major Battle with date
········ Proclamation Line of 1763

4

John Paul Jones

"I Have Not Yet Begun to Fight"

| 1777–1779 | During the Revolutionary War |

John Paul Jones stood on the deck of the *Bonhomme Richard*, shouting orders to his frantic, struggling sailors and Marines. The night sky was alight with **muzzle flashes** as two great ships blasted away at each other in deafening **broadsides**. He could not know that this fight would stamp his name upon the pages of history and that he would someday be known as the Father of the American Navy.

muzzle flashes: Light from the sudden release of a firearm

broadsides: Firing from all guns on one side of a ship at the same time

apprenticing: Working for another, usually without pay, to learn a trade

He had started life as the son of a poor Scotsman. His sailing career had begun as a voyage out of the English town of Whitehaven on the *Friendship*, **apprenticing** for Captain Benson. He first trod the deck of a sailing ship at age 13. In the years that followed he saw service on various merchant vessels and gradually rose in rank.

His big break came unexpectedly. Serving as third in command aboard the ship, John Jones was suddenly thrust into the top job. Yellow fever attacked the crew.

The captain and the one seaman above Jones in rank died. Now Jones, barely in his twenties, found himself responsible for sailing the ship and its valuable cargo safely into port. It wasn't easy, but he did it.

He was rewarded. The grateful Scottish owners of the ship made him permanent captain. In addition, they gave him ten percent of the cargo.

America's War Heroes

It was a considerable fortune for a man so young. He went on to lead two successful voyages to the West Indies before running into trouble.

He had ordered a sailor **flogged** for **inciting** mutiny. Unfortunately, the man died a few weeks later and Jones was tried for charges related to unnecessary cruelty. The charges were dismissed, but the man's family was wealthy and influential. Jones had made some powerful enemies. On a later voyage, a **mutinous** crew member attacked the captain and died at the edge of Jones' sword. His reputation severely damaged, he left his fortune behind and fled to the colonies in America.

flogged: Punishment with a whip or a stick

inciting: Causing or instigating

mutinous: Sailor who is willfully disobedient and causes trouble

He found a new home in the New World. Within a few years, America was at war with England fighting for independence. John Paul Jones joined her **fledgling** navy and quickly distinguished himself as a fighting commander. He had captured many English ships, both military and merchant vessels. He had even raided towns on the British coast. The new United States called him a hero. In England, he was portrayed as a pirate. On September 23, 1779, the lookout in the **crow's nest** shouted that a ship was in sight. Indeed, there were many ships. It was a merchant **convoy** off the coast of Flamborough Head. The mighty British frigate *HMS Serapis* and the 22-gun *Countess of Scarborough* were guarding the merchant ships. As

fledgling: Inexperienced, brand new

crow's nest: A shelter or platform fixed near the top of the mast of a vessel as a place for a lookout to stand

convoy: Group of ships traveling together for safety

they spied the *Richard*, the two gunboats **maneuvered** themselves

> **maneuvered:** Skillfully arranged in a strategic position to gain an advantage

between the American ship and the merchants. As the merchant ships made their escape, Jones ordered his crew to approach the *Serapis* and do battle.

The Battle

It was a little after 7 p.m. when the two ships drew within pistol shot of each other. In the gathering darkness, British Captain Pearson of the *Serapis* called out to the *Richard*. What was the name of this vessel that approached His Majesty's ship? To what nation did she belong?

Boom! The answer was the first shot in the greatest battle of John Paul Jones' career. Suddenly the darkening sky was lit up by the flashes of broadsides. Balls and shrapnel ripped across the decks, tearing through sails and rigging and leaving sailors squirming on the wooden decks in pain. Battle cries blended with the shrieks and groans of the wounded. **Powder monkeys** dashed to serve the gunners. The constant blast of cannons and small arms was deafening.

> **powder monkeys:** Boys employed on a sailing warship to carry powder to the guns

The two ships appeared fairly evenly matched, each having about 300 men aboard. Their weaponry was similar also, with about the same number of cannons. However, the *Bonhomme Richard* had a disadvantage that was not evident to the eye. Unlike the *Serapis*, which had been designed for fighting, the *Richard* had been a French merchant ship that had been fitted with cannon and other equipment for fighting. The ship could not move as efficiently as the *Serapis*. Some of her guns were second-hand 18-pounders that were old and had been taken out of service in the French navy.

Within the first half hour of fighting, two of the old 18-pounders blew up, killing several of the sailors nearby. Suddenly Jones realized he could not win a cannon duel against the *Serapis*. He would have to find another way to fight, or he would have to strike his colors and surrender. Surrender was not an option.

Grappling was the answer! Jones ordered his men to ready the **grappling hooks** and ropes. Scrambling to obey, sailors leaped to grab their equipment. Pearson quickly saw their intent and moved his more mobile ship to stay out of reach. At the same time, he continued to blast the slower vessel.

grappling hooks: Device with iron claws attached to a rope in order to tie up to another ship or dock

There was no doubt the *Richard* was taking a beating. As the pounding continued, her sails were in tatters and many lines were cut. The proud flag she bore was torn away and left floating in the Atlantic waves. The ship floated helplessly, struggling to return fire. Water began to run through holes in the hull. The *Bonhomme Richard* was sinking.

The British captain, seeing that Jones' flag was down, shouted through a megaphone, "Have you struck?" It did indeed look as if Jones was surrendering to end a hopeless battle.

John Paul Jones was in the habit of winning his battles and he had no intention of losing this one. One of his sailors later remembered the reply Jones shouted back to the British captain: "I have not yet begun to fight!"[12]

A Chance at Last

Still, it looked hopeless. Cannon balls had broken holes in the *Richard's* hull below the water line and it was becoming harder and harder to handle the ship. Just then, a jib-boom on the *Serapis* got tangled in the *Richard's* rigging, binding the two ships together, at least for a moment. This was the chance Jones had been waiting for. Shouting to his men for help, he grabbed a rope and tied it between the rail of his ship and that of the *Serapis*. Working frantically among the bullets flying from both directions, they soon had the ships tied securely together.

Most of Pearson's big guns were still in action and they did terrible damage at this close range. Huge holes were blown in the *Bonhomme Richard's* hull and many of the ship's guns were destroyed. Only three of the nine-pounders on the quarter-deck still fired. Two of these were loaded with **grapeshot** to drive the British sailors from the deck. That was the only way a boarding crew from the *Richard* could cross over and seize the *Serapis*.

grapeshot: Ammunition consisting of small iron balls fired together from a cannon

rigging: Masts, cables, chains, and ropes that hold up the sails

grenades: Small bombs thrown by hand

Jones knew his ship was sinking. However, he still had some tricks in his bag, and he was determined to board the *Serapis*. He placed men up in the **rigging** to fire muskets down on the enemy and to throw **grenades**. High on a yard arm, William Hamilton could look almost straight down on the deck of the *Serapis*. Most of the enemy sailors were cleared from the deck now. No one was shooting at him as he carefully tossed his grenades toward an open hatch in the deck below.

One toss hit **pay dirt**. It dropped neatly through the hatch and ignited a charge of gunpowder placed for loading into one of *Serapis'* big guns. The effect was devastating. As the powder blew up, it scattered burning sparks that set off other charges nearby. Many British sailors were killed and wounded. Some leaped into the sea to **quench** fires on their clothing. Five guns were put out of action.

pay dirt: Struck its target

quench: Put out, extinguish

Bonhomme Richard's gun decks were now splintered. Most of the British shots passed straight through without touching anything. Most of Jones' guns had been silenced. There were many fires to be extinguished and the hold was filling with water. Some of the pumps were out of action.

Seeing the end was near for the *Bonhomme Richard*, Pearson decided to send a boarding team. Ever thinking, Jones had prepared for this. He had a force of men in hiding to repel the boarders. They were quickly driven back to their own ship. At the same time, the few remaining guns on the *Richard* had damaged the mast on the *Serapis* and it was now leaning over on the rigging on Jones' ship.

Now the American ship was settling so quickly in the water that the British prisoners captured in previous battles were in danger of drowning. Without waiting for orders, the master-at-arms released the prisoners. Free from their place below decks, they could have helped *Serapis'* crew to overrun the American ship. Thankfully, quick-thinking Commodore Jones urged them to save their own lives by putting all their energy into working the three remaining pumps.

Now the *Alliance*, another ship in Jones' squadron, came to assist. Her broadsides slammed into the *Serapis*. Caught between this new enemy and the unrelenting fire from Jones' sinking vessel, Captain Pearson knew his position was hopeless. With his own hands he hauled down the British flag from the leaning mast.

The gallant *Bonhomme Richard* had won the battle, but it would be her last. For two days Jones and the crew struggled to save the ship, but the pumps could not keep up with the torrents of water rushing in. At last, they gave up, cut the ropes tying the two ships together and watched the *Richard* slowly sink beneath the waves of the Atlantic.

Repairs were made to the *Serapis*. The wounded on both sides were cared for. The British seamen were confined in the hold as prisoners. Then the sails were raised, the anchor pulled up, and John Paul Jones sailed away toward a friendly French seaport and into history.

The War of 1812

The war of 1812 was a conflict between the young United States of America and the British Empire. The war began in 1812 and ended in 1815. The two nations had been troubled by tensions over control of certain areas of North America ever since the end of the Revolutionary War. In addition, the British navy was interfering with trade between the United States and France. A major issue was the taking of American sailors from American ships and impressing them into service in the British navy under the pretense that they were actually British citizens.

Sea power gave Britain a great advantage in the war, but both sides won significant victories in battle. During the war, the British burned much of Washington, D.C. Neither side was a clear victor in the war, but the British navy stopped the **impressments** of American sailors and the United States continued its expansion into new territory to the west. An interesting historical fact of the War of 1812 is that the last great battle was fought after the war

impressments: Forced to serve in the military

actually ended. This was the British assault on New Orleans in which American forces under Andrew Jackson turned back British troops led by General Edward Pakenam. This victory was an important factor in the election of Jackson as President of the United States in 1828.

5
Stephen Decatur
and the Pirates

February 1804	During the War with the Barbary Pirates

Barbary Pirates

Young Lieutenant Stephen Decatur stood on the deck of the *Intrepid*, a mild breeze blowing through his dark, curly hair. His nerves were on edge as he and his crew of Marines floated ever closer to their target, the United States ship *Philadelphia*. It was around seven o'clock on a February evening in 1804. He was on an **ironic** mission. Decatur was sailing a small ship built by his enemies to destroy a larger ship built by his fellow Americans.

Decatur had already proven his skill and courage in naval battles against the French. French ships had been attacking American ships trading with the British. The French and British nations were at war with each other at the time, so the French considered trading with the British an offense against France. They did not officially declare war against America, so history refers to the conflict as the **Quasi-War**.

Now another war was being fought. For centuries, **Muslims** from several nations on the north shore of Africa called the Barbary Coast had been attacking ships and coastal towns, killing and capturing innocent people. Ship cargoes had been taken and sold by the cruel raiders, and hundreds of thousands of prisoners taken. Ship crews and villagers were sold as slaves. Historians believe that over a million slaves were captured by these Barbary Pirates.

ironic: Strange, unexpected

Quasi-War: An undeclared naval war fought from 1798–1800 between the United States and the French First Republic or "Pirate Wars"

Muslims: Followers of Islam

Many nations lost people to the pirates. Across the Mediterranean Sea and from Italy to Ireland, the raiders sacked ships and burned

towns, taking men, women, and children captive. Sometimes they murdered people by the thousands. A Muslim commander named Dragut attacked the town of Vieste in Italy in 1554. He took over 6,000 captives to sell as slaves. He did not have room in his ships for the rest of the people of the town, so he had them killed. Five thousand innocent people died in this mass murder.

Wealthy people who were taken captive by the Muslims were sometimes ransomed by their families. Others were forced to gain their freedom by converting from Christianity to Islam. Most of those captives remained slaves for the rest of their lives, never to see their homes and families again.

This raiding had been going on for centuries when America made a treaty with the Barbary nations so their ships would not be attacked. The United States had to pay millions of dollars for the pirates to let their ships pass in peace. When Thomas Jefferson became president, he decided that America would no longer be **blackmailed**. Ships were built and equipped with powerful cannons. Across the Atlantic they sailed, determined to end the raiding and murder.

blackmailed: To demand money in exchange for not attacking them

Outsmarting the Pirates

On October 31, 1803, the American **frigate** *Philadelphia* had been captured by the Muslims

frigate: A sailing ship with one gun deck

in Tripoli harbor. The ship had been sent as part of a seven-ship squadron to punish the pirates but had the misfortune to get grounded on some rocks. Chasing an enemy ship into the harbor, she had run into water that was too shallow for her great size. Captain William Bainbridge had tried every trick he knew to lighten the ship so she could float off the rocks. He had even thrown most of his cannons overboard. Nothing worked. The *Philadelphia* was surrounded by enemy ships and captured. The crewmen were made prisoners.

The pirates intended to free the *Philadelphia* and use her to attack the other American ships. Commodore Edward Preble, the commander of the squadron, did not intend for this to happen. He and his officers consulted together to come up with a plan to take the *Philadelphia* back or destroy her.

It was young Lieutenant Decatur who suggested a clever but dangerous plan. An attack force could be concealed in another ship pretending to be a Muslim vessel. Sailing close to the *Philadelphia*, the ship could get in position for the men on board to leave their hiding places and climb aboard the grounded ship. They would then kill or capture the enemy sailors on board. But how could the Americans disguise one of their own ships to fool the pirates into allowing them to approach?

They would not have to. Decatur pointed out that the American squadron had captured a Barbary ship in a recent battle. It still had the same kind of sails that propelled the enemy ships. If the American fighters stayed out of sight and the approach was made in the evening when the light was poor, it just might trick the pirates.

The other officers agreed that the plan was brilliant. Now, who would get the honor of commanding this mission? All of Preble's young officers volunteered, but he decided that since the idea had been Decatur's, the lieutenant should be the man to execute it. The stage was set for Decatur to step into the pages of history as the first great American naval hero since the Revolutionary War.

Although in prison, Captain Bainbridge had also thought of destroying his captured ship and wanted to help prepare for this sneak attack. Since they were hoping to get a ransom from the American government for the release of Bainbridge and his men, the Muslims had allowed Bainbridge to send letters to Commander Preble. Of course, the letters would be read by the pirates before being taken out to the American ship. The prison where the American officers were held had a view of the harbor. Bainbridge could give Preble important information about the location of the *Philadelphia* and the harbor defenses. This must not be allowed to happen.

But Bainbridge outsmarted his captors. He wrote the information on the letter in lemon juice. The pirates could read the part of the letter that was written in ink, but the lemon juice became invisible when it dried. It was not until Commander Preble heated the letter over a candle that the secret words became visible. Now Decatur's plan could be made even more effective!

Firing the Ship

It was a four-day sailing trip from the squadron's position to Tripoli's harbor, and a storm had delayed the small Barbary ship, which had

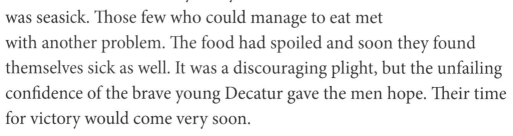

been renamed the *Intrepid*. Anchored ten miles off the Tripoli coast to ride out the storm, the sailors and marines waited and suffered. Conditions in the little ship were awful. Small and fragile, the little craft pitched and rolled in the gale waves. It was overcrowded and infested with rats and mice. Nearly everyone was seasick. Those few who could manage to eat met with another problem. The food had spoiled and soon they found themselves sick as well. It was a discouraging plight, but the unfailing confidence of the brave young Decatur gave the men hope. Their time for victory would come very soon.

Now the *Intrepid* was entering Tripoli harbor. The athletic young lieutenant peered through the gathering dusk, every nerve tingling. The harbor could become a death trap if the enemy figured out that the approaching boat held American fighting men. It was a difficult harbor to navigate, with shallow places where his ship could get stuck just as the *Philadelphia* had. If they were recognized, the only escape route out of the harbor passed within a thousand yards of the fort's cannon.

As a caution against that, the men on the deck of the *Intrepid* were dressed like the native **Tripolitans**. Most of the raiders would remain below deck until the moment of the attack. The ship was guided by a Maltese pilot named Salvador Catalano who spoke the local Arabic language. The plan was for Catalano to call out to the guards on the *Philadelphia*, asking for permission to tie up to the larger ship.

Tripolitans:
Persons from Tripoli

As the little *Intrepid* came within shouting distance, Catalano launched his story. Their ship had been damaged in a storm, he told them. They had lost their anchors and needed to tie up for the evening. Permission was granted. Slowly the *Intrepid* approached the side of the much larger ship.

Suddenly, one of the guards looked down on the *Intrepid's* deck and noticed that the ship still had her anchors. Realizing the trick, he shouted "Americanos!"

The guards were thrown into confusion. Some of them believed the warning and others did not. Then Decatur gave the command: "Board!" The Marines came swarming up from the hold of the ship and scrambled up the side of the *Philadelphia*. One member of the boarding crew would one day recall, "The effect was truly electric. Not a man had been seen or heard to breathe a moment before; at the next, the boarders hung on the ship's side like cluster bees; and in another instant, every man was on board the frigate."[13]

Decatur had ordered the men to keep the noise at a minimum, so the fighting was done not with guns but with swords, knives, and spears. Taken by surprise, the few guards who put up a fight were soon killed or captured. The rest jumped into a small boat and rowed away or jumped overboard and swam to shore. The fight lasted only ten minutes and only one American was wounded. So far, so good.

Now the *Philadelphia* must be put to the torch and their escape made on the *Intrepid*. Decatur issued orders to his panting men and they split into squads to start fires. Fuel they had carried on the *Intrepid* was brought aboard and placed in the cockpit, storerooms, and gunroom. When all was ready, Decatur ordered "Fire!" All over the ship, sailors touched off the blazes.

Quickly, the Marines cut the ropes that held the two ships together, then climbed back down to the deck of the *Intrepid*. Striding calmly along the deck amid the smoke billowing dark out of every hatchway, Decatur strained his eyes in the gloom to be sure every American was safe and back on his ship. Indeed, the fire had spread so fast that some men were nearly trapped in the burning hold. At last, Decatur left the deck of the *Philadelphia*. He was the last man off.

But the danger from fire was not over. The *Intrepid* was still very close to the *Philadelphia* and one sail was dangerously near the flames. Desperately the crew fought to get their ship out of harm's way. They used long oars to push the *Intrepid* away from the blazing hulk. But the *Intrepid* kept drifting back. Quickly Decatur sent a team to take a rowboat from the ship and tow the ship into position where the sails could catch the light breeze. Meanwhile, Muslim cannons from the shore started booming and small arms began sending a hail of bullets toward the retreating Americans.

The Americans worked with a vigor inspired by danger. Using both oars and sail, they guided the little ship toward the Western Passage and safety. Behind them, the harbor darkness seemed to turn to daylight from the inferno

America's War Heroes

aboard the *Philadelphia*. Raging flames leaped toward the sky as the great ship burned. Finally, the *Intrepid* reached the dark sea and safety. Forty miles away, her sister ship, the *Siren*, would report that the glow from the fire was still visible at six o'clock the next morning.

The war to stop the crimes of the Barbary pirates was just beginning. But young Lieutenant Stephen Decatur had struck a powerful blow on behalf of his country. It would not be long before President Thomas Jefferson's great goal would be accomplished, and American ships would once more sail through the Mediterranean in safety.

News of Decatur's triumph electrified America. Nations across the world realized that the young and tiny American navy was a force to be reckoned with. Stephen Decatur would go on to win other laurels in other battles, rising quickly in rank and fame, but the burning of the *Philadelphia* would stand always as his most famous adventure.

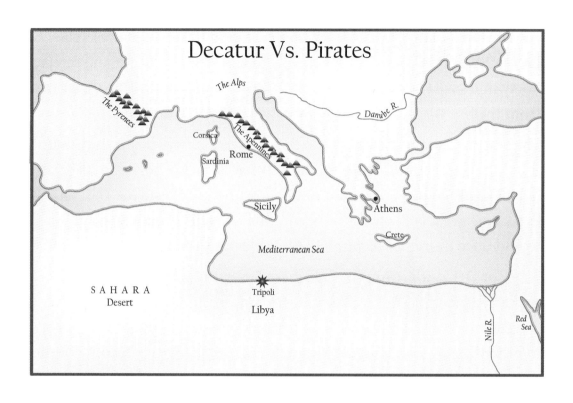

6

David Farragut – Boy at Sea

1812	War of 1812

David Glasgow Farragut seemed to have been born with seawater in his veins. As long as he could remember, he had wanted to be a sea captain like his foster father. He did not have to wait many years for his chance. His mother died when he was a small boy and young Farragut was adopted by Captain David Porter, a longtime seafaring man. Captain Porter promised that his young charge would get his chance at life on the ocean.

One day young David had the chance to meet the Secretary of the Navy. The great man was pleased with David's desire to serve in the Navy of the United States. He was impressed as he asked the boy many questions and received intelligent answers. His eyes were kind as he

> **midshipman:**
> Naval cadet

said, "My boy, when you are ten years old I shall make you a **midshipman** in the Navy."[14]

Boy Seaman

What a proud moment for a little boy! Today such a promise would seem like a fairy tale. But in those days before the War of 1812, boys as young as ten often served on United States ships. They were given schooling at the same time as they learned the duties of seamen. Young David was given his appointment early. He was only nine when it came. Much learning, adventure, danger, and hard work lay ahead. At the end of that road lay great honor. David Farragut would one day be the very first Admiral in the United States Navy. His humble beginning would be to serve under his foster father, Captain Porter, on the frigate *Essex*.

France and England had been at war with each other for many years. British ships attacked French ships whenever they met at sea. They would also attack any vessel going to or from ports in France. This meant that American ships were attacked by the British even though the two countries were not at war. Worse than this, the British claimed that they had the right to stop American ships and search them to see if any English deserters were aboard.

This did not stop them. Many times each year, American sailors on their own ships were accused of being deserters from the British navy and taken to serve on British vessels. It was nothing but kidnapping.

All this was terribly wrong, but the American government tried to settle the matter peaceably. England, in contrast, was very proud. The British had been master of the seas for a very long time and they felt that no one could stop them from doing whatever they wanted to do.

War of 1812

Finally, the problems had gone so far that the Americans saw no choice but to fight. War was declared on June 18, 1812. The government fitted out a squadron to cruise the Atlantic coast and protect American ships from the attacks of the British.

Due to the fact that the *Essex* was not ready to sail with the others, Porter had been ordered to finish preparations as quickly as possible and then join the **squadron** in the Atlantic. These were the days before there were ship's radios. It might not be possible to find the other ships in the squadron. If that happened, Captain Porter was to do whatever he thought best.

squadron: A group of warships

Finally, the *Essex* was ready. Down the Delaware River she sailed, flying a **pennant** that read, "Free Trade and Sailors' Rights." These were the causes for which Captain Porter and his men were ready to fight.

---

pennant: Flag flown from the masthead

By the captain's side stood little midshipman David Farragut, proud of his captain, his ship, and his neat new uniform. Now he felt like a real sailor at last.

The *Essex* cruised around the Atlantic for several months. Porter and his crew captured several English ships, but their squadron could not be found. Captain Porter decided to take his ship to the Pacific. They set sail for a trip around Cape Horn.

The passage around Cape Horn is a dangerous one. The *Essex* was a good, solid ship and she had a brave captain and a well-drilled crew. The men worked hard at their fighting skills and all of them were good swordsmen. All were well prepared to board another ship in battle. Sometimes Captain Porter ordered fire drills. He would sound a false alarm of fire on board, sometimes even causing a cloud of smoke to go up from somewhere on the ship. Each man was trained in exactly what to do in any kind of an emergency. The men of the *Essex* felt they were prepared to be able to navigate sailing even around Cape Horn, which could be quite a challenge.

Unfortunately, storms struck as the ship rounded the Cape. The weather was very cold. For three weeks the ship was pounded by furious winds and waves. Food and water began to run low. Each man received only a little bread and water each day. Young Farragut was getting a taste of what it really meant to be a seaman.

Finally, the Cape was put behind them and they sailed north into better weather along the west coast of South America. They stopped at an island near the coast of Chile. Here the hungry sailors went ashore with their guns in search of meat. They found wild hogs and horses living on the island and killed some of them in order to survive.

The *Essex* cruised the lovely blue Pacific for months. They captured several English vessels and stopped to talk with American whaling ships. Some of these ships had been at sea for a long time and had not heard of the war between America and England. They needed to be warned.

On one lonely island they found a strange post office. It was nothing but a box, nailed to a tree. In that box passing ships would leave letters and messages which would be picked up by other vessels which happened to be going in the right direction. It must have taken many weeks or months for such messages to be delivered.

This island became a refuge for the *Essex* for some time. On the island the crew found wild fruit. They killed wild pigeons to be made into pies by the ship's cook. There were plenty of turtles, so turtle soup was often on the menu. Midshipman Farragut ate heartily along with the other seamen. Then, in May of 1813, the *Essex* sailed away from the friendly island. The men were rested and well-fed. They had taken aboard plenty of fresh water and preserved food. It was time once again to do battle.

David in Charge

They were about to be put to the test in a fierce fight. Weeks and months went by on the blue water as the *Essex* sighted and captured more English ships. It was then that David Farragut got his first taste of command.

When an enemy ship was captured, the captain and the crew were sometimes locked below decks in the hold of the ship. At other times, they might be allowed to freely move about the ship as long as they caused no trouble. At some time after the battle, they would be exchanged for American prisoners who had been captured by the British.

One of the captured English ships was to be sailed to the port of Valparaiso on the coast of Chile. Captain Porter put Midshipman Farragut in charge of a crew of men borrowed from the *Essex* to do the job. David was only 12 years old when he took on this great responsibility.

The English captain was a gray-haired seaman with many voyages behind him. He did not like taking orders from a boy, and a small boy at that. He threatened to shoot any man who obeyed David's orders and started down below to get his pistols. Young David had the loyalty of his crew and did not intend to have the ship taken away from him. His Captain had ordered him to deliver the prize to Valparaiso and that was exactly what he intended to do. He sent a message to the English captain assuring him that if he caused any further trouble he would be thrown overboard. There was no more trouble.

David rejoined the *Essex* in time to help Captain Porter sail to some distant islands for refitting. Food and water had to be replenished and the ship's carpenter had work to do repairing battle damage.

Approaching one of these islands, the ship was greeted by a group of natives in a canoe. The people were decorated all over with tattoos and bright feathers. They invited the sailors to come ashore. Fruit and other provisions were available, they said, and so it was.

Six weeks were spent refitting the *Essex*. During this time, the sailors got some much-needed rest on the island. David and the other boys of the crew caught up on their studies with help from the ship's chaplain each day. After school was over, they were free to visit their new friends among the islanders.

The American boys took lessons from the islanders as well as the chaplain. They were taught to throw a spear and walk on stilts. Swimming lessons were given by experts. The island people seemed to move about in the water as easily as on land. Even the babies were like ducks, floating easily on the surface of the water.

You have heard it said that all good things must come to an end, and that is what happened to the men on the *Essex*. In December of 1813, they sailed for Valparaiso.

The Loss of the *Essex*

One February day in 1814, the *Essex* was lying at anchor in the harbor of Valparaiso. Many of her crew were on shore. Suddenly two English war vessels appeared over the horizon and entered the harbor. They approached the *Essex* as if they meant to attack. They had no right to do this because the nation of Chile was neutral — they were not at war with either America or England.

Captain Porter was alarmed. The bold approach of the *Phoebe* and the *Cherub* indeed had the look of an attack. The *Phoebe* glided toward the *Essex* until she was within 15 feet of her side. But the American captain was not to be **intimidated**. He hailed the *Phoebe*: "If you touch a single yardarm, I shall board you instantly!"[15]

The *Phoebe* passed on by, saying nothing in reply. Later, both British ships anchored at the entrance of the harbor, creating a barricade between the American ship and the open sea. The *Essex* was a prisoner.

intimidated: Frightened into changing one's mind or plans

After several weeks, Captain Porter determined to make a break for the open sea. He set all sails and made for the mouth of the harbor, hoping to slip past the British ships. To his dismay, a gale was blowing and suddenly a loud snap was heard. The main top mast had broken and now came crashing down. Sails and sailors were thrown into the water amidst a tangled mass of rigging.

Escape was now impossible. Huge waves drove the wounded *Essex* toward the shore. Dragging her anchors, she finally stopped just a few hundred yards short of the beach. With no way out, there was nothing left to do but fight.

The Americans were in a desperate position. The *Essex* had only four guns that could shoot as far as the cannon on the English ships. The Britishers took a position beyond the range of most of Porter's guns and sent broadside after broadside into the *Essex*. The Yankee sailors never had a chance.

Porter and his crew were strong and brave men. They would not go down without a fight. So they gave the British everything they had until 124 American soldiers lay dead or wounded on the decks. Finally, they hauled down their flag.

During all this carnage the little officer David Farragut was showing himself as brave as any of the grown men. He seemed to be all over the ship, carrying messages for the captain across decks slippery with blood or running as a powder monkey, carrying ammunition for the guns as the shells burst around him. Captain Porter was so impressed with David's conduct that he mentioned the boy's courage in official **dispatches** to the government.

dispatches: Messages

Work was not over when the battle ended. The wounded men were removed to the shore and the surgeons went about their desperate work to save lives. Alongside them little David Farragut worked as well, doing anything he could to assist the doctors, bringing water to the wounded men and preparing bandages. It was long and exhausting work. Years later Farragut was heard to say, "I never earned Uncle Sam's money so faithfully."[16]

Finally, the American prisoners were put aboard an unarmed ship and paroled. They were to be set free in exchange for their promise that they would not again fight against the British until they were exchanged. Then they set sail for home, arriving in New York harbor on July 7, 1814.

David Farragut's first mission was over. It had certainly been a lively one.

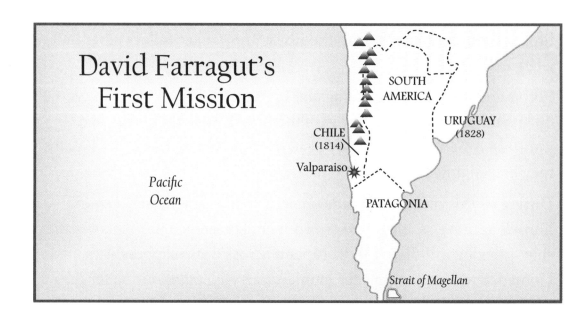

David Farragut's First Mission

Pacific
Ocean

SOUTH
AMERICA

CHILE
(1814)

Valparaiso

URUGUAY
(1828)

PATAGONIA

Strait of Magellan

The Civil War

The deadliest war in terms of American deaths took place on American soil in the years 1861 through 1864. More Americans died in the War Between the States than in any other war in history. Eleven southern states had seceded from the Union and formed a new nation, the Confederate States of America. The Confederacy elected Jefferson Davis, a former U.S. Senator, as President. The United States government, led by President Abraham Lincoln took the position that states did not have the constitutional right to leave the union, and sent armies south to force the seceding states to return.

Much of the reason for **secession** was the conflicting interests of the industrial north and the agricultural south. The northern states had a larger population, and so had more Congressmen in the House of Representatives. This meant that the northern states could pass laws that were favorable to themselves, but caused problems in the southern states. Some of these laws involved tariffs, charges placed on goods brought into the U.S. from other countries. Tariffs caused the price of these goods to be higher in the United States. For example, a tariff on wool hurt the South more than the northern states because the northern states produced more wool and so needed to buy less from England.

secession: To leave a political union

Another cause of the war was the issue of slavery. Slavery had existed all over the world for thousands of years. In the early days of America most Americans believed slavery was a bad thing and should be abolished. However, the slavery problem was a hard one to solve. Some farms depended on slave labor. Abolitionists believed that the slaves should be set free immediately and given all the rights of American citizens. Others argued that suddenly setting free millions of people who had not had the chance to learn how to take care of themselves would create disastrous problems. Radicals on both sides refused to compromise. Though every other English-speaking nation had managed to get rid of slavery without a war, America was doomed to four long years of suffering and bloodshed. Even then, the repercussions of slavery continued well into the 21st century.

America's War Heroes

7

Mosby – The Gray Ghost of the Confederacy

1862–1865	During the Civil War

He Was Called the Gray Ghost

John Singleton Mosby had begun his career with the Confederate army at the beginning of the war as a **private**. He soon found himself in the

private: Lowest rank of enlisted personnel

cavalry: Soldiers who fought on horseback

cavalry, and before long he had attracted the attention of the top cavalry officer, General "Jeb" Stuart. Mosby's daring and effectiveness as a scout for Stuart led to a command of his own. Though that command would never be a large one by the usual standards of war, the brilliance of its leader would quickly make it a force to be reckoned with. The name of Mosby would become a source of terror to the Union army and a beacon of hope to the South.

Mosby's Rangers

Mosby and his men were a **"partisan"** unit. Like the **privateers** of the sea, these free-wheeling rangers were by law permitted to keep some of the spoils of war which they captured from the enemy. They were soldiers of the regular Confederate army, but they were

partisan: Member of a fighting force that fights in secret

privateers: Armed ships owned and operated by private individuals authorized for use in war by the government

required to provide their own horses. They served without pay.

John Mosby himself was not fighting for profit. He and his closest allies in the company were dedicated to creating so much trouble in the enemy's rear flank that soldiers would have to be drawn from the front to defend many points against the partisans. That was their mission. The opportunity to gain a free horse or some needed harness attracted the loyalty of other southerners who were willing to fight the invaders from the North but felt they could not afford to leave their families and farms uncared for. If they could strike a blow for freedom and at the same time acquire things needed at home, they could be persuaded to join Mosby.

The work of the Mosby men was not to engage large numbers of the enemy and destroy them. They were a small, fast-moving force that could swoop in, capture prisoners and horses, then disappear. Like Mosby's hero, Francis Marion (known as the Swamp Fox of the American Revolution), they struck suddenly and often at night. Often the partisans would **dismount**, sneak up quietly on foot and capture a Union picket outpost with little or no bloodshed. Sometimes they would storm on horseback into a large **Yankee** camp at midnight with blood-curdling yells and revolvers blasting. Striking where they were least expected, Mosby's little force kept the rear guard of the northern army off balance and nervous. Knowing Mosby could strike at a hundred different points, Union commanders had to invest thousands of soldiers to defend against "Mosby's Confederacy." That meant thousands who could not help with the battles against Robert E. Lee at the front.

> **dismount:** Get off their horses

> **Yankee:** Northern sympathizers

Mostly, Mosby's Rangers (also called Mosby's Raiders) **disrupted** supply lines, captured Union couriers, provided intelligence to the regular Confederate army, and generally became a thorn in the side of federal officers operating in northern Virginia.

> **disrupted:** Destroyed or interrupted

Mosby's Rangers fought without a regular headquarters or long-term camps. After a raid, the men scattered and found a meal and a bed in the home of some sympathetic Virginians. When their leader had conceived a plan for their next battle, riders were sent throughout the countryside with a call to arms. As their record of success grew, more men joined them. But at the same time, there was opposition.

Some in the South believed that partisan warfare was not very effective. Mosby's was not the only partisan band operating against the Yankees. It was also known that some of these bands had become outlaws, preying on civilians as well as military targets. Mosby was afraid that he might lose his command if the Confederate government decided that partisan companies were not worthwhile. Men and horses were in short supply in the regular army. It was possible the government might decide that Mosby's troops would be more useful in defending Richmond, the Confederate capitol. That must not happen. There was too much valuable work to be done in the enemy's rear flanks.

A Daring Plan

The Rangers needed to show their worth. The country and its leaders needed to hear of something big — something shocking — that Mosby's men had accomplished. They needed to pull off a major exploit that would become front-page news. After considerable brainstorming, Mosby had the answer. He would capture Wyndham.

Colonel Sir Percy Wyndham was commander of a cavalry brigade including the Fifth New York, Eighteenth Pennsylvania, and First Vermont units of the Union Army. He was the highest-ranking cavalry officer in northern Virginia, and he hated Mosby. The Gray Ghost had been a constant thorn in Wyndham's side, capturing his men and stealing his horses. Time and again the partisan leader had slipped through Wyndham's fingers when it seemed sure that his capture was **imminent**. Sir Percy had sworn to bring Mosby's troublesome career to an end, but so far, he had failed.

Part of the reason for this failure was Sir Percy's background. A former British army officer, Wyndham was well-schooled in the European style of fighting. He understood the **tactics** of large armies of men facing each other over an open field. But he was **baffled** by enemies who struck when least expected and then scattered. Their headquarters could not be found and captured because they had no headquarters. Their supply lines could not be cut because there were no supply lines. Instead, it was the Union supply lines that were being disrupted. Now, Mosby was **scheming** to invade their headquarters as well.

The man who made such a daring plot possible was a new recruit to the Rangers, a Union deserter. This man, Sergeant James F. Ames, turned against the Union cause and the Fifth New York Cavalry for reasons that were never explained. Many of Mosby's men did not trust Ames. What if he were a Union spy?

Mosby decided to put Ames to the test. He would accompany the Rangers on a raid. He would be unarmed. Mosby himself would be riding right behind Ames, ready to shoot him if he tried anything **treacherous**.

imminent: Sure and about to occur

tactics: Strategies, plans

baffled: Perplexed

scheming: Plotting, planning

treacherous: Involving betrayal

But when the Rangers attacked, Ames jerked a Union soldier off his horse, tore the man's sword out of his hand, and furiously assaulted every Yankee within reach. Mosby never learned the reason for Ames' hatred of his former brigade, but on this night all suspicion in the minds of the Rangers **vanished**. Ames was warmly welcomed into the company.

vanished:
Disappeared

Mosby found Ames to be a godsend. The man knew the location of every Union force in Fairfax County. In addition, he knew a route by which the partisans could pass through the whole system of Wyndham's cavalry posts all the way to his headquarters at Fairfax Courthouse. Big Yankee, as he had been nicknamed by the Rangers, would be their guide to catching Wyndham unawares.

The town was occupied by five or ten thousand Union troops, but this was considered no problem by Mosby. That very fact meant that the Yankees would not be on guard. They would never dream that a small company of Confederates would dare come within miles of their location. The stage was set for the great triumph Mosby needed. When he captured the man who had been pursuing him, Mosby would become a hero throughout the South and the value of partisan fighters would be established. No one could argue with success. At the same time, the feat would create a panic on the Union side. The North would clearly see that their rear flanks needed more protection. More Yankees occupying the rearguard meant fewer to fight Lee at the front.

A Surprise Raid

On the evening of Sunday, March 8, 1863, Mosby led 39 men off on a daring mission. It was the largest group of men that had followed him to date. It was a drizzly night with snow melting underfoot, a perfect night for a surprise raid. Along the road between Centreville and Fairfax, they cut the telegraph line. Leaving the road, they headed through the woods toward Fairfax Courthouse. Only Mosby and his guide, Ames, knew their destination.

When they rode into the courthouse square, the others realized where they were. Whispers of alarm buzzed through the company. Mosby was calm. "That's right," he told them, "we're in Fairfax Courthouse, right in the middle of ten thousand Yankees. But don't let that worry you. All but about a dozen of them are asleep."[17]

Then he gave his orders. Men were sent to surprise and capture guards. The telegraph wires were cut and the operator taken prisoner. A group went to Colonel Wyndham's quarters but found that he had gone to Washington. Rangers went to the stables, leading horses out to meet new masters. Mosby took a few men and went to the headquarters of General Stoughton (Stau•ton), the commanding officer. He knocked loudly on the door with his revolver butt.

A window opened on the floor above. "Who's there?"

"Fifth New York Cavalry with a dispatch for General Stoughton," was the reply.

A man holding a candle appeared to open the front door. "I took hold of his nightshirt, whispered my name in his ear, and told him to take me to General Stoughton's room," Mosby recalled. With a revolver pointed at his face, the officer was quick to obey.

Entering Stoughton's room, they found the general sleeping soundly. "There was no time for ceremony, so I drew up the bedclothes, pulled up the general's shirt, and gave him a spank on his bare back, and told him to get up," Mosby remembered.[18] Grouchily, Stoughton asked what was going on.

"Have you heard of Mosby?" the raider asked him.

Stoughton replied with excitement, "Yes! Have you caught him?"

"No, he has caught you."[19]

Mosby told the general to dress quickly, and the raiders prepared to leave.

So far, no shots had been fired and the thousands of northern soldiers surrounding Mosby's men were still sound asleep. However, there were still many miles between the Rangers and safety. Quietly they herded their captured horses and prisoners along, passing close by Union **picket lines**. Thanks to the cut telegraph lines, no one outside Fairfax Courthouse knew of the raid. All the Rangers made it safely back to Confederate lines. They had swept up General Stoughton, two other officers, 30 enlisted men, and 58 horses. It had been a fruitful night.

picket lines: Small units of soldiers watching for an enemy advance so they can warn others

Mosby had accomplished much of what he had hoped for. Overnight he found he had become a Confederate hero. He had proven the value of partisan warfare and now he knew that he would not be recalled to the regular army. He was promoted to major. He was authorized to raise a larger group of partisans, and with them he proved to be a thorn in the side of the Union army through the rest of the war.

Finally, Robert E. Lee was outnumbered and forced to surrender. However, John Mosby did not surrender his command. He simply disbanded them and told them to go home. They disappeared from active service, but they and their colorful commander still live in history.

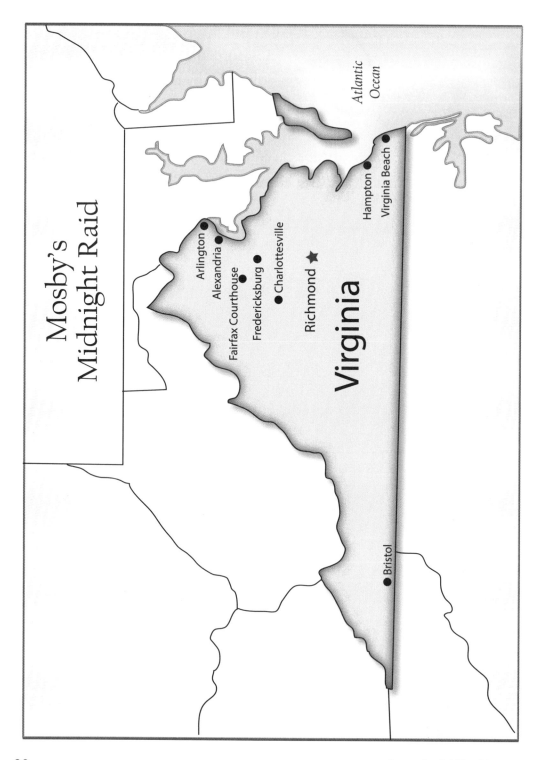

Mosby's Midnight Raid

Virginia

Atlantic Ocean

Arlington
Alexandria
Fairfax Courthouse
Fredericksburg
Charlottesville
Richmond
Hampton
Virginia Beach
Bristol

World War I

Early in the 20th century there was a great deal of tension between several of the great national powers of Europe. The spark that ignited open warfare was the 1914 assassination of Archduke Franz Ferdinand, heir to the throne of Austria-Hungary, by a Bosnian Serb. Austria-Hungary held the nation of Serbia responsible and although there was an attempt to settle the issue through diplomacy, it failed. Soon the two nations were at war, with other nations joining one side or the other until a global conflict was under way.

The Central Powers consisted of Austria-Hungary, Germany, the Ottoman Empire, and Bulgaria. Opposing them were the Allied Powers: France, Belgium, the British Empire, and nearly twenty other nations who joined them. In 1917, the United States joined the Allies. American power broke the stalemate between the two sides and Germany and her allies were driven back. The war continued until November 11, 1914, when an armistice was signed between the Allies and the Central Powers. Under a series of treaties, especially the Treaty of Versailles, Germany was required to pay for damages resulting from the war.

America's War Heroes

8

Sergeant York –
Unlikely Hero

October 8, 1918	The Argonne Forest during World War I

Acting corporal Alvin York flexed his muscles and shrugged his pack straps into a more comfortable position on his broad shoulders. The Tennessee boy had come a long way from the cabin in the hills. His memory of growing up on a quiet farm with his ten brothers and sisters seemed almost a dream as he surveyed the grim scene before him.

This was not green Tennessee. This was the Argonne Forest in France. The First World War had rudely torn Alvin from his mountain home and now he and his comrades in arms found themselves in a ruined woodland on a dark, damp day. Shattered tree trunks sprouted toward the gray sky, their branches gone or tattered by exploding shells in the recent fighting. The ground was plowed by artillery blasts and the rain had turned the raw earth to sticky mud that pulled at a man's leggings and made his boots slip underfoot as he struggled to fight his way forward.

Ahead of them lay a good chance for violent death. Surveying the valley in front of him, York listened to the whistle and boom of artillery shells and the chatter of distant machine guns. The Germans were dug in on the hills across the valley. They were well settled in trenches and **foxholes**. York's unit had been ordered to silence those guns. However, advancing against machine guns without armor was a job to make the bravest man pause. Already thousands of American, French, and British soldiers had ended up face-down in the Argonne mud trying to do what York and his comrades had been ordered to do. For weeks they had marched and fought. They had slept in muddy trenches and were tired and dirty most of the time. Their boots were seldom dry. Their feet were often blistered and **trench foot** had taken

foxholes: A hole in the ground used by troops for shelter

trench foot: A painful condition of the foot caused by long exposure to water or mud

many men out of action. These young soldiers, most of them with very little experience in combat, were driving the enemy out of France. But many of them were dying in the process. All of them were suffering.

Alvin's Youth

Alvin York was as able as any man to face the hardships of war. Growing up in a mountain cabin, he and his family struggled to make a living. Hard farm work and hunting in the wooded hills around Pall Mall had made him tough and strong. He was gifted with a steady hand and a sharp eye. When Alvin fired his rifle, he seldom missed.

He had always been a fighter. He had a reputation for being quick with his fists and for liking a good scrap. Though he was known to attend church fairly often, he remained a hard-headed country boy. His mother prayed for her boy faithfully, but wild friends were a strong force pulling him away from a wise path.

Then everything changed for Alvin York. Christ found Alvin and Alvin found pretty Gracie Williams, a neighbor girl who had no patience for his wild lifestyle choices. She would be waiting for him when the war was over.

Confused

However, a battle of another kind had to be fought before Alvin would face the Germans. As he progressed in his new life, his study of the Bible changed his way of thinking. He had always been a fighter. The Scriptures taught him that he must love his neighbor and even his enemies. When his **draft card** came in the mail calling him to war, his heart was torn. He wanted to serve his country, but "I was worried clean through," he said. "I didn't want to go and kill. I believed in my Bible." The draft card asked the question: Do you claim exemption from draft (specify grounds)? Alvin's answer was simple and clear: "Yes. Don't want to fight."

draft card: A card sent by the federal government telling someone they must enlist in the military, often done in wartime

His request to be classified as a **conscientious objector** was denied. He **appealed** the decision. His appeal was denied as well. Alvin York entered the army in 1917 at Fort Gordon, Georgia.

conscientious objector: Someone who is opposed to bearing arms in the military because of moral or religious principles

In basic training, Alvin was a mystery to his friends. Here was a strong, tough young man from the mountains of Tennessee whose skill with a rifle was amazing. His shooting proved to be almost miraculous. His rifle was like a best friend. He had taken it apart and put it back together so many times that "I could almost do it with my eyes shut." Yet he did not want to go into combat! "One moment I would make up my mind to follow God, and the next I would hesitate and almost make up my mind to follow Uncle Sam. Then I wouldn't know which to follow or what to do. I wanted to follow both. But I couldn't. They were opposite. And I couldn't reconcile them **nohow** in my soul."

appealed: To apply to a higher authority to reverse a decision

nohow: In no way

America's War Heroes

Alvin had long conversations with his battalion commander, Major Braxton. Braxton was a dedicated Christian who knew the Bible well. He showed Alvin that fighting is not always wrong. Alvin came to see that God sometimes wanted men to fight for causes that were right. York said that Buxton read other parts of the Bible which he said proved that a man under certain conditions could go to war and fight and kill and still be a good Christian.

Alvin was given a 10-day leave to go home and pray for wisdom. When he returned to the 82nd infantry, he was convinced. God wanted him to fight for his country. It was this decision that would write the name of Alvin York into American history.

The Battle

That September, Alvin and his comrades fought in their first major battle. They won the battle, and Alvin won a promotion to corporal. After this battle came a series of battles all along the Western Front. They lasted from September 26, 1918, until the end of the war on November 11, 1918.

Now it was October 8th, and the Americans were advancing, determined to drive the Germans from their positions. As the young men looked toward the opposite hill, the valley between seemed a hundred miles across. They knew that the enemy guns would be pouring hundreds of bullets toward them every minute once they started moving.

Years later, Alvin would remember that advance: "The Germans got us, and they got us **right smart**. They just stopped us dead in our tracks. Their machine guns were up there on the heights overlooking us and

well hidden, and we couldn't tell for certain where the terrible heavy fire was coming from. . . . And I'm telling you they were shooting straight. Our boys just went down like the long grass before the mowing machine at home. Our attack just faded out. . . . And there we were, lying down, about halfway across [the valley] and those German machine guns and big shells getting us hard."

Alvin's squad, led by Sergeant Bernard Early was ordered to take out the machine guns dug in up there and spitting death toward the American lines. Twisting and dodging, using the few remaining bushes and tree trunks for cover, the men of Early's squad advanced. Corporal York, the **cagey** Tennessee hunter, had convinced Early that the only chance they had to succeed was to work their way around the nearest German unit from behind. Suddenly they stopped dead in their tracks

as they topped a rise and found themselves face to face with the headquarters of a German unit. For just a second the German soldiers were completely stunned. The Americans were surprised too, but reacted just an instant faster. They covered the Germans with their rifles and shouted at them to surrender. Hands shot up all over the camp. "**Kamerad!**"

Now the **Yanks** had a double problem on their hands. Alvin, breathing hard, looked around at the prisoners they now had to guard. How could they do that and still advance up the hill and attack the machine gun nests?

Suddenly the air was filled with the roar of guns and the zipping of bullets. Americans and prisoners alike hit the ground as it seemed that every weapon in Europe had been turned on their position. Sergeant Early and a few of his men had been hit and were out of action. Early ordered Alvin York to take charge. Alvin told some of his men to guard the prisoners while he and the others returned fire.

Later, he would write in his diary: "And those machine guns were spitting fire and cutting down the undergrowth all around me something awful. And the Germans were yelling orders. You never heard such a racket in all of your life. I didn't have time to dodge behind a tree or dive into the brush. . . . As soon as the machine guns opened fire on me, I began to exchange shots with them. There were over 30 of them in continuous action, and all I could do was touch the Germans off [shoot them] just as fast as I could. I was sharp-shooting … All the time I kept yelling at them to come down. I didn't want to kill any more than I had to. But it was they or I. And I was giving them the best I had."

His best was good enough. Leaving his men in the German headquarters to guard the prisoners and fight back as best they could, Alvin fought his way up the hill through a hail of bullets. With only half a clip of bullets left in his rifle, he switched to an automatic pistol and fought on. All the while, he was calling on the Germans to surrender. He did not want to kill any more men than he was forced to.

Suddenly a German lieutenant and five soldiers vaulted out of a trench 25 yards away and ran toward York in a bayonet charge. This was indeed a desperate situation. Alvin resisted the natural urge to shoot at the man at the front of the charge. If the leader went down, the others would take cover and start shooting. At such a close distance, Corporal York would have no chance to live. They could not miss him at that range. But the old hunter's instinct came to the rescue. Just as he had hunted flocks of turkeys back home, York shot the man at the rear of the charge first. He went down, and the hunter aimed at the man just ahead of him. It was over in seconds, and the German lieutenant was practically on top of Alvin when a pistol bullet ended the war for him.

A German major had witnessed this display of marksmanship and he now called out to Alvin. If he would stop shooting, the major said, he would call on the rest of the Germans on the hill to surrender. Alvin agreed and the major gave a whistle. All over the hilltop German soldiers left their machine guns and came out of their trenches with their hands up. But how could one man control such a mob? Alvin stuck his pistol into the major's back and assured him that if one German made a false move, the major would pay with his life.

Alvin marched his prisoners back to the headquarters where his squad was waiting. He ordered the Germans to carry the wounded men and started the group marching back to the American lines. By the time their journey was over, Alvin York had single-handedly captured 132 German soldiers.

Back at headquarters, Brigadier General Lindsey congratulated him: "Well, York, I hear you captured the entire German army." York replied that he "only" had taken 132.

America's War Heroes

Alvin C. York was promoted to sergeant for his bravery. In addition to his prisoners, he was given credit for 28 enemy soldiers killed and 35 machine gun nests taken out of action. He would receive the Medal of Honor from the American government and nearly 50 other awards from several allied countries. Always humble, he gave all the glory to God: "So you can see here in this case of mine where God helped me out. I had been living for God and working in the church some time before I come to the army. So I am a witness to the fact that God did help me out of that hard battle; for the bushes were shot up all around me and I never got a scratch. So you can see that God will be with you if you will only trust Him; and I say that He did save me."[20]

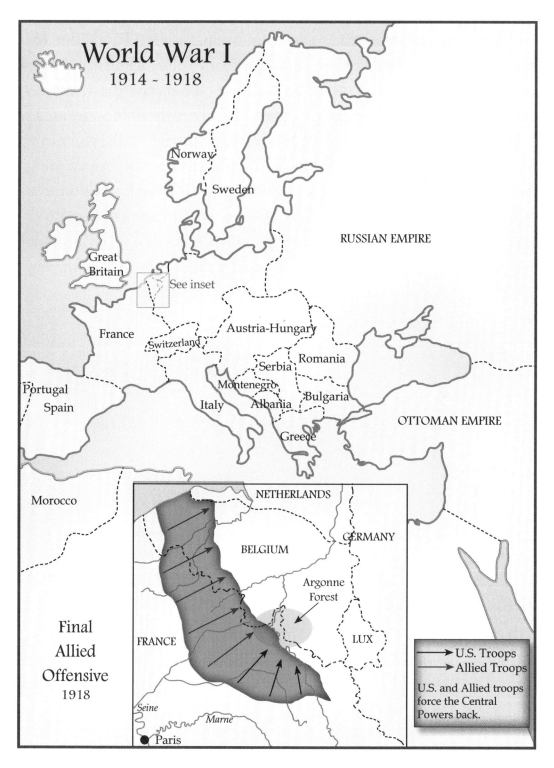

World War I
1914 - 1918

Norway

Sweden

RUSSIAN EMPIRE

Great Britain

See inset

France

Switzerland

Austria-Hungary

Romania

Serbia

Montenegro

Portugal

Spain

Italy

Albania

Bulgaria

Greece

OTTOMAN EMPIRE

Morocco

Final Allied Offensive 1918

NETHERLANDS

BELGIUM

GERMANY

Argonne Forest

FRANCE

LUX

Seine

Marne

Paris

→ U.S. Troops
→ Allied Troops

U.S. and Allied troops force the Central Powers back.

World War II

World War II was a worldwide conflict that involved nearly all the countries of the world. Many historians say the war began with the German invasion of Poland in 1939. However Japan, Germany's ally in the war, had been expanding its territory in Asia and the Pacific years before that, including the invasion of Manchuria. Italy was also an ally of Germany, and as the war progressed several other nations joined them in what became known as the Axis powers. The ambition of Adolph Hitler, Germany's chancellor, to control Europe was the driving force that brought on thc war.

Against the Axis powers stood the Allies. The main allied nations were the United Kingdom, France, the Soviet Union, and the United States. At first, the war mostly consisted of Germany's aggressive actions against other European nations. However, when Japan struck Pearl Harbor and other American bases in the Pacific in a devastating surprise attack on December 7, 1941, the United States declared war on Japan. In turn, Germany and her allies declared war on the United States.

The war in Europe ended in May 1945, when Germany surrendered to the Allies. Japan surrendered in August of that same year, ending the war in Asia and the Pacific. Historians estimate that between seventy million and eighty-five million people died in World War II, most of them civilians.

9

Jake Deshazer – From Prisoner to Preacher

| 1940–1945 | During World War II |

It is one of the most amazing stories of World War II. Two men from different countries went to war as enemies and finished their lives as friends.

It was Sunday, December 7, 1941 — a peaceful, sunny morning in the Hawaiian Islands, while much of the rest of the world was at war. So far, the United States had managed to stay out of the fighting, although she was supplying millions of dollars in aid to England to help defend the island nation from Germany. The Hitler war machine was grinding its way across Europe, killing thousands and destroying entire towns in the process. England and her allies were praying for their American friends to finally give up on their hopes for peace and leap into the conflict with guns blazing. So far, that had not happened. But then everything changed.

Surprise Attack

Just before eight o'clock in the morning, the blue Hawaiian sky was suddenly dotted with lines of small dark spots. As the lines grew closer, the sound of engines was heard and the spots took shape. They were airplanes. Sailors on the dozens of American warships floating quietly on the blue water of Pearl Harbor looked up curiously to see the huge and unexpected squadron that had appeared.

Then suddenly the leading planes dove toward the earth. This was no routine exercise or training mission. Someone noticed the red circle painted on the planes. They were Japanese!

This was very strange. Surely it could not be an attack. America and Japan were at peace. In fact, at that very moment, Japanese diplomats were in Washington, D.C. to arrange a treaty between the two nations.

Why then were those planes over Pearl Harbor today and why did their approach suddenly look like an attack formation? There were only seconds in which to wonder. Then the harbor exploded.

In the lead plane, Captain Mitsuo Fuchida shouted, **"Tora! Tora! Tora!"** into his radio microphone. It was the order to attack, given in Japanese.

> **Tora! Tora! Tora!:** Literally means "tiger" in Japanese, but implied a lightning attack

The whistle of falling bombs was heard and then the ear-splitting explosions. Boom! Boom! Geysers of water shot up into the air as American sailors shouted warnings to each other and ran to man their guns. Several ships were already damaged and burning before the first shots from the ships began to answer the Japanese attack. Men poured from below decks to man battle stations, many of them partially dressed as they were tragically called away from sleeping in on this sunny Sunday.

Within minutes, black clouds of oily smoke boiled up from several ships. Wave after wave of Japanese planes dove, dropped bombs and torpedoes, then moved on to attack nearby Hickam Field and other targets. At Hickam, nearly every American plane was destroyed before it could get off the ground to go after the Japanese bombers. Before the day was over, nearly 3,000 Americans lost their lives, and the U.S. Navy suffered devastating losses in ships and planes. Pearl Harbor had suffered the most terrible attack in American history.

The news of the attack began to spread. Telephones and radios carried the message around the world. A little later that morning, a special alert came to an army base in Alaska where a young American soldier was peeling potatoes.

Revenge

It was Jake DeShazer's turn for **K.P.** duty. Every low-ranking soldier had to take his turn now and then at helping to cook, clean up, and wash dishes. Today was the day for this boy from Oregon.

K.P.: Kitchen patrol

Jake had grown up in a home in which the Bible was honored and prayer was a daily practice. Jake loved his family. His mother and stepfather loved him and Jake loved them and his siblings. But though Jake respected their faith, he decided it was not for him. He had other things that interested him more than religion.

Now thoughts of peace and love were the farthest thing from his mind. He jumped to his feet, threw the potato he had been peeling across the room like a bullet, and shouted, "Those Japanese are going to pay for this!"

That day there was born in Jacob Daniel DeShazer a flaming hatred for the Japanese people. As details of the Pearl Harbor disaster flowed in, he and his buddies grew angrier and angrier. It had been a sneak attack by a supposedly friendly nation. As the day wore on, radio reports told of the terrible damages and loss of life. Their imaginations ran wild with thoughts of other young Americans blown to

America's War Heroes

pieces, bleeding, burned to death. They swore that when the chance came to take Japanese lives in revenge, they would rush to volunteer.

Jake did not have long to wait. A few weeks after the Pearl Harbor attack, word came that the Army was looking for volunteers for a top-secret mission. To DeShazer it sounded like a chance to strike a blow at the enemy. He volunteered.

What Jake did not know was that the American government was planning an air strike on Japan. The Japanese thought that they were safe from aerial bombing because their navy controlled most of the Pacific Ocean. Their government had assured them that no enemy country could ever send bombers to Tokyo or Hiroshima or Kyoto. Bombers could not carry enough fuel to cross the entire ocean. Huge aircraft carriers that could move planes closer to Japan would be held at a distance by the Japanese Imperial Navy.

Wheels were turning in the minds of American military leaders and politicians. Japan had dealt a devastating blow to America's naval power. At the same time, they had shaken U.S. confidence to the roots. The leaders knew that some great show of force was needed to restore the confidence of their people. They needed to see that **Uncle Sam** could strike back at an enemy with **devastating** force. Congress had declared war on Japan and her ally, Germany. There was a long war ahead. America's home team needed a decisive victory, even a small one. The plan for the Doolittle Raid was almost ready.

Uncle Sam: Term meaning the United States government

devastating: Highly destructive

Top Secret Mission

A plan was made to bomb the home islands of Japan. If the mission could be accomplished, it would restore American hopes and show the Japanese that their rulers were lying to them about how easy victory was going to be. When word came that volunteers were needed for a top-secret mission, Jake DeShazer was quick to answer the call. Surely this would be a chance to kill Japanese. Very soon Jake found himself in training as a **bombardier**.

In April 1942, Jake and his buddies were on the aircraft carrier *Hornet*. Now they learned more about the mission. Sixteen planes and 80 men would drop bombs on five Japanese cities. Jake DeShazer would drop his bombs on Nagoya (ˈnä-gȯ-yä). He could not wait.

bombardier: Member of a bomber crew responsible for releasing bombs

On April 18 the B-25 medium bombers left the *Hornet's* deck and headed for Japan. All the planes were soon over their target cities. Jake and his fellow crewmen cheered as they dropped their 500-pound bombs. This was a visit Nagoya would not soon forget. They roared away, avoiding the anti-aircraft fire from below. Successful mission! Now the hard part came.

The B-25s could not carry enough fuel to return to the carrier. Therefore, the plan was to fly to mainland China. There they would land if possible before their fuel ran out. If that was not possible, they were to parachute and find friendly Chinese people to help them make it to American lines. It was a reasonable plan, but it did not work for Jake.

Jake's plane did not make it to friendly territory. The Japanese had invaded China and controlled much of the countryside. Jake and his fellow crew members waited tensely as their engines droned on and their fuel slowly ran out. At last, the pilot gave the word to bail out. They were out of gas.

It was long after dark that the little crew left their plane and hung silently in the night sky below their canopies of silk. It seemed a long time before the ground came rushing up to meet Jake and he found himself alone, shaken up, and out of breath on the grass. Looking around, the dim light showed that he had landed in a graveyard.

Captured

The next day, Jake and his comrades were captured. They had not managed to fly far enough to get beyond Japanese-held territory. The eight men were sent to Japan for trial as war criminals. Three of them were executed and the rest were sent to prison in China.

The next three-and-a-half years were a nightmare for the young Americans. They were tortured, starved, and beaten. Of the 40 months they spent in prison camps, they endured 34 months in solitary confinement. Their cells were scorching hot in the summer and without heat in winter. The men were sick much of the time. Time crawled by, and with every new day, Jake DeShazer hated the Japanese more. Later he would say that his hatred nearly drove him crazy.

Solitary confinement is a dreadful torture. Hours seem like months with nothing to do and no one to talk to. Many people go insane in such conditions. Jake and the other prisoners sat in their lonely cells, unable to see through the high windows and only allowed out for exercise for a few minutes each day. They shared their homes with rats, lice, and bugs. They begged their guards for books to read to make their prison bearable. Books written in English were scarce in China.

Finally, some books did come into the prison. One of these was a Bible. Jake knew a little of the Bible from his time at home. Now he was hungry to explore it for himself. Hour after hour he read the Scriptures. In the books of prophecy, he saw that the prophets kept writing about a Man who was to come to the earth to do great things. He would show people the path of life, and then die to pay for their sins. He would provide a way for them to be forgiven.

After a few days new light began to dawn in Jake's soul. He saw that he was a sinner and that he needed forgiveness. He learned that he needed to repent of his sin and confess with his mouth that Jesus is Lord. There in his small, miserable cell Jake bowed his head and met the Jesus of whom he had been reading. He became a changed man because of his new relationship with Christ.

His life did not change in every detail right away. Soon, however, he found that he could forgive his Japanese guards for the terrible things they were doing to him and his friends. Even with the beatings, starvation, and sickness, he began to say like Jesus, "Father, forgive them for they know not what they do." He began to speak kindly to the guards when they came around to check on the prisoners. Slowly, the guards began to be less harsh with the prisoners.

At long last, the war ended, and Jake and his friends were set free. Back home in Oregon, Jake surprised his friends and family with his plans for the future. If any of them doubted that he was a new creature in Christ, they must have soon become convinced. Jake said that he was going to Bible college to prepare to be a missionary. He was going to Japan. He would start sharing the gospel in the city of Nagoya!

Missionary to Japan

While in college, he met a cheerful young lady named Florence. Florence also wanted to be a missionary. In a few years they were married and settled in Nagoya. The Japanese people were eager to hear the strange story of a former enemy who had become a friend. Jake wrote a tract titled, *I Was a Prisoner of Japan*. He and his team gave away thousands of them. Many people received Christ as they heard from Jake how God had forgiven him and given him the power to forgive his enemies.

But the job of reaching millions of Japanese was a huge task. "We need God to work in a miraculous way," Jake told Florence one day. "I'm going on a long fast to beg the Lord to show us a miracle for Japan."[21] He fasted for 50 days. At the end of it, he looked like a skeleton. But God honored his prayers in a powerful way.

One day shortly after ending his fast, Jake heard a knock at his door. When he answered it, a Japanese man was standing there. Jake invited him in. The man explained that he was a veteran of the war and had recently become a Christian. He wanted to meet Jake because his salvation had come through reading Jake's tract, *"I Was a Prisoner of Japan."* The man was Mitsuo Fuchida — the pilot who had led the attack on Pearl Harbor!

Jake and Mitsuo became lifelong friends, often sharing the gospel together in Japan. All because one man purposed to show forgiveness to his enemies, thousands of Japanese people were saved as Jake preached the gospel with his former enemy! Mitsuo traveled throughout America and Europe sharing his testimony. Many of the people who heard him preach were American men who had fought against Mitsuo Fuchida's country in the war. In an amazing demonstration of His grace, God used Jake's story of forgiveness through Mitsuo's life to show both the Japanese people and American veterans the way to salvation and to help heal the wounds of war.

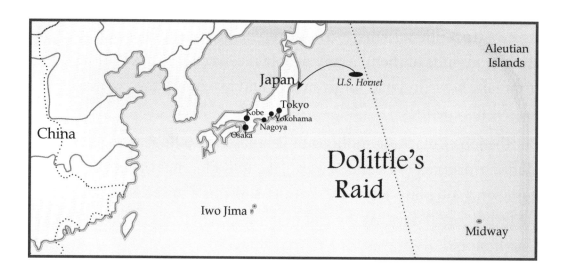

10

Desmond Doss –
The Unarmed Hero

1942–1944	During World War 2

World War II was coming to an end. The Germans were only a few days away from surrendering in Europe. Now the Allies were closing in on Japan. War in the Pacific, however, was different. After the Battle of the Bulge, the German army's last major offensive, the Nazi forces had grown weaker and weaker. But the Japanese were being driven across the Pacific, steadily retreating toward their homeland. America and her allies were slowly grinding their way along, skipping some Japanese-held islands and taking others after nightmare battles against enemies who would rather die than surrender. As the war moved closer to Japan itself, the resistance grew ever more determined. Back home, Japanese women were being trained to fight with spears even as the government was **brainwashing** its people to believe that the Americans would be

> **brainwashing:**
> Telling someone wrong information to deceive

unspeakably brutal if they ever landed on Japanese soil. People were prepared to jump off cliffs while holding babies in their arms when the Americans approached. The Japanese were going to be hard to conquer.

War in the Pacific

The island of Okinawa was to be the scene of one of the bloodiest battles of the war. Located only a few hundred miles from the home islands of Japan, it was considered to be an ideal location to be used in preparing for the final attack on that country. Only 60 miles long and 20 miles wide, that small strip of real estate would cost the lives of 12,000 Americans, 100,000 Japanese, and around 100,000 civilians. The island was

honeycombed with caves which General Mitsuru had expertly equipped to serve in his defenses. The weeks of blasting from big artillery on American navy ships off the coast had hardly made a dent in the Japanese works. At the same time, attacks on those ships by **kamikaze** (kom-y-kah-zee) planes had taken a heavy toll on American ships and men.

> **honeycombed:** Filled with cavities or tunnels

> **kamikaze:** Desperate military maneuver

After months of "softening up" by American land and air forces, the land invasion began. It was launched on April 1, 1945, when U.S. ground troops landed at Hagushi, on the west coast of the island. When night came, General Buckner's troops were 50,000 strong on a five-mile **beachhead**. Japanese resistance had so far been less than on some other islands, but it was just the beginning.

Company B of the 77th Division would see some of the most horrible fighting on Okinawa. Among the men of Company B was young Desmond Doss of Lynchburg, Virginia. Doss was a skinny, soft-spoken southerner who had been working in a naval shipyard early in the war. When he was drafted in 1942, Doss could have easily gotten a **deferment** because he was working in a war-related industry. He had declined.

> **beachhead:** A defended position on a beach taken from the enemy by landing forces from which an attack can be launched

> **deferment:** Postponement from the draft

The Conscientious Objector

Even though he had been raised with religious beliefs that taught that killing was wrong, Desmond was a patriotic American and wanted to serve his country in the war.

He did not refuse to be enlisted, but he wanted to be a combat medic rather than a fighting man. He believed the war was a **just** war and was willing to do his part. For him, that meant saving lives rather than taking them.

Though the army considered him a conscientious **objector**, Doss was still required to undergo basic training along with the other soldiers. He appealed to be allowed not to take weapons training. The army officials were very much against this, but finally granted the request. After much conflict, he was even permitted to attend religious services on Saturday, which was the practice of the church he attended.

just: Morally justifiable

objector: A person who for reasons of conscience objects to complying with a particular requirement, especially serving in the armed forces

exemplary: Outstanding

Boot camp was even more unpleasant for Doss than for the other soldiers. At that time, conscientious objectors were often thought of as cowards and traitors. The other men did not seem to see that a medic in the army needed more courage than the average soldier because he had to go into combat with no weapon to defend himself. Doss was harassed and insulted by the other men. When he knelt to pray by his cot, other men threw boots and other items at him. One soldier even threatened to kill him once they got into combat. He was bullied by his commanding officers as well. There was something in Doss that would not be conquered. He held fast to his Bible and his faith. He became an **exemplary** soldier.

Attempts were made to throw Doss out of the army. His commanding officers tried to discharge him for mental illness, but he refused. One officer tried to **court martial** him for refusing to hold a gun. That attempt failed as well.

In 1944, Doss shipped out for the Pacific as a combat medical corpsman. The 77th landed on Guam in July 1944. In that bloody battle, his comrades from boot camp

> **court martial:** To try him before a military court for offenses against military law

quickly changed their minds about wanting to kill him. Here was the skinny boy from Virginia, acting as if he really was mentally ill! He was running from foxhole to foxhole, bullets flying all around him as he bandaged wounds, applied **tourniquets**, and dragged bleeding men to safety. Before it was over he was awarded the Bronze Star, a high award for courage. It seemed they had been mistaken about the bravery of their Bible-toting medic. When they fought at Leyte, Doss was a

> **tourniquets:** Tight bandages to stop major blood flow

hero again. He was awarded a second Bronze Star. However, it was at Okinawa that the name Desmond Doss would be written into American history.

Okinawa

The majority of the Japanese army was fortified on the southern end of the island. It was a region of rough limestone hills, very good for building defenses. American forces had cut the island in two and were

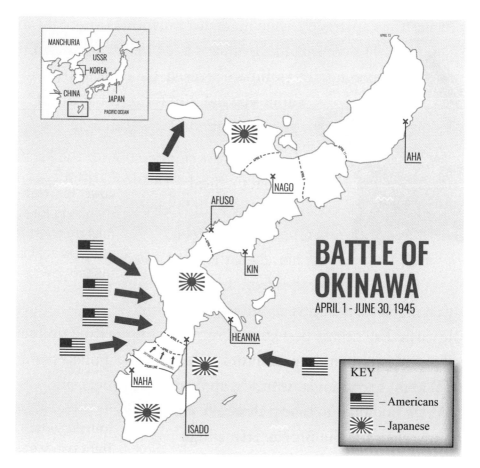

The following labels appear on the map:

MANCHURIA
USSR
KOREA
CHINA
JAPAN
PACIFIC OCEAN

AHA

NAGO

AFUSO

BATTLE OF
OKINAWA
APRIL 1 - JUNE 30, 1945

KIN

HEANNA

NAHA

ISADO

KEY
— Americans
— Japanese

now fighting their way southward. One important location was called
the Maeda Escarpment. Desmond's company was to be part of the
force that must take it.

An escarpment is a steep slope with a cliff at the top. If an escarpment
is used as a defensive position, it can be very hard to attack. It is always
difficult for soldiers to fight going uphill, and the cliff at the top of
Maeda was 30 to 50 feet tall. It would have to be climbed using nets. It
must be captured. From the top of Maeda, the Japanese could see the
ocean on both sides of the island and far out to sea. It was easy to keep
an eye on what the Americans were doing.

Captain Vernon explained to his men what they were up against. He told them that two divisions had been cut to pieces trying to take that hill. At that, the men of Company B looked at each other. They had been in frightening situations before, but this was something special. Some of the men looked at Desmond. His faith had been an encouragement to them before, and the presence of a brave medic was very important. It could mean the difference between life and death for a wounded soldier.

In the darkness of early morning, Company B moved into position at the base of the cliff. It seemed to be a fairly safe location. There were huge boulders there, creating holes where men could take cover if enemy fire came near. Some of the boulders hid openings to caves that went deeper into the earth. Later that day, two men explored the area and decided where the cliff could be climbed. From the top they could see several **pillboxes** and gun positions. They sent for equipment to help climb the cliff and for more weapons, including **flamethrowers**. The attack was set for the next day.

> **pillboxes:**
> Concrete dug-in guard posts with holes from which to fire a gun

> **flamethrowers:**
> A weapon that sprays out flaming fuel

At daybreak, two squads scaled the cliff. At the top, they found hundreds of rocks which they used to build a wall to shield them from enemy fire. One by one, they pushed the rocks forward into position. By staying low they stayed out of sight of the enemy. No bullets came their way. Looking around, Desmond could see why the position was so important to the army. From here he could see American ships landing supplies and men. From this location, the Japanese could keep an eye on everything the Americans were doing.

Whump! Without warning, an explosion sounded on the other side of the rock wall. A mortar shell! These mortars could fire nearly straight up into the air, landing shells behind walls to kill the men on the other side. It was only a matter of getting the range and that would take only a few trial shots. Hastily the exposed Americans scrambled back down the cliff.

Captain Vernon reported back to headquarters that the company had pulled back. He received orders to attack again the next day. Company A would attack also, to the left of Vernon's company. Large cargo nets, the kind men used to climb on and off ships, would be brought to make the climbing easier. Desmond was one of the three men who climbed the cliff again to hang the nets in position.

Finally, the order was given to climb. The first objective the men had was a large pillbox on the hill above that the enemy was using as an observation post. From there, the Japanese were able to direct their artillery fire, such as the mortars that had driven Desmond and his friends from the cliff the previous day. This concrete structure had to be destroyed for the Americans to move forward. Desmond volunteered to go along. Lieutenant Gornto, the leader of the mission, told Desmond that it was a dangerous job and that he would not be required to go. He told the lieutenant that he felt he should because he may be needed. Then he made a request. He told the lieutenant that he believed that prayer was the biggest lifesaver there was, and that every man should have a word of prayer before he set his foot on the rope ladder to go up that cliff. He meant that each man should pray silently by himself, as Desmond often did when facing danger.

But Gornto called all the men together and told them that Doss was going to lead them in prayer as a group. No one objected. So, even though there was no time for preparation, Desmond simply poured out his heart to God for himself and his comrades. He asked for wisdom, both for the leaders and the men. He asked that if it were the Lord's will, they all would come back safely. And then he asked God that if any of them were not prepared to meet their Maker, they would make peace with Him through prayer before they started up the cliff. For a moment after he said "Amen," the group remained still and silent. Desmond felt sure that every man was praying sincerely. Then they signaled to A Company and both companies started up the cliff.

Reaching the top, the men moved steadily toward the pillbox. Private Black's **bazooka** blasted a hole in the side of the concrete bunker. Then a soldier threw a **satchel** charge through the hole. It exploded and a flamethrower sent a flood of fire into the pillbox. The work was done.

bazooka: A short-range tubular ammunition launcher

The unit moved on. Japanese soldiers threw hand grenades from their hiding places and a furious fight began. But prayers were answered. The only wound the company received was in a sergeant's hand. He had been struck by a piece of flying rock.

satchel: An explosive on a board lifted with a rope

Finally, they were relieved by another unit, but Desmond stayed behind. He felt that he might soon be needed. He was. Cries of "Medic!" began to sound from multiple directions. Soon Doss was crawling all over the hilltop, patching up wounded men. If they could move, he would help them back to the top of the cliff and help them climb down the net. All the while, a hail of Japanese gunfire made it seem as if all of them must be hit sooner or later.

A soldier drew back his hand to throw a grenade, but just at that second a bullet hit him, and he stood stunned. The grenade blew up in his hand, taking the hand off and wounding three nearby soldiers. Desmond dropped to his knees among them, struggling to care for four injured men as bullets swept the hilltop. Soldiers threw hand grenades over his head to keep the Japanese from shooting him. Quickly he stopped the lieutenant's bleeding from his shattered hand and his other wounds, then dressed the wounds of the other three. Two of the men could crawl, so Desmond sent them back to make their way down the cliff. An infantryman ran up to help the third man get to the rear. Then Doss grabbed the lieutenant by the collar and dragged him a few inches at a time back toward the cliff.

"Medic!" A shell had landed in a machine gun nest, killing one soldier and blowing the lower leg off another. Zigzagging, Desmond ran and jumped into the hole. He bound the wounded leg tightly, then began dragging the man to the net.

Day and night, the battle continued. At last, the Americans were ordered to withdraw. But there were still wounded men who could not help themselves. Desmond Doss refused to leave them. Even when he was the last able-bodied man on the escarpment, he kept treating wounds and lowering injured men down the cliff with a rope wrapped around a stump. All through this time,

Japanese bullets from above and American bullets from below made every step a hazard. Doss would not quit. Each time he got a man to safety he would pray, "Lord, help me to find one more."[22] When he could no longer find wounded men to rescue, he was credited with having saved 75. For this amazing heroism, he would receive the Congressional Medal of Honor.

Desmond Doss was finally wounded and picked up by other medics. Before they could get him to an aid station, he saw a man who seemed to be in worse shape than he was and he rolled off the stretcher, demanding that the medics take the other man first. They came back for him hours later.

Doss survived the war, but his wounds took months to heal. When he returned home, he was treated like royalty by his fellow Americans. Publicity and parades were not to his liking. He had a young wife waiting at home and what he wanted most was to get back to her and start the family they had both dreamed of and that is just what he did.

Glossary

Alleghenies: The western part of the Appalachian Mountains; extending from northern Pennsylvania to southwestern Virginia

appealed: To apply to a higher authority to reverse a decision

apprenticing: Working for another, usually without pay, to learn a trade

baffled: Perplexed

bayonet: A blade fixed to the muzzle of a gun

bazooka: A short-range tubular ammunition launcher

beachhead: A defended position on a beach taken from the enemy by landing forces from which an attack can be launched

blackmailed: To demand money in exchange for not attacking them

bluff: Trick

bombardier: Member of a bomber crew responsible for releasing bombs

booty: Enemy equipment or property captured on the battlefield

brainwashing: Telling them wrong information to deceive

brigadier general: An officer of the army, who holds a rank junior to a major general but senior to a colonel, usually commanding a brigade

Britishers: Native inhabitants of Great Britain

broadsides: Firing from all guns on one side of a ship at the same time

brow: The top part of a hill or the edge of something high such as a cliff or rock

buckskin: Made from the skin of a male deer

cagey: Cautious

cavalry: Soldiers who fought on horseback

cocky: Arrogant

commission: A formal document issued to appoint a named person to high office

conscientious objector: Someone who is opposed to bearing arms in the military because of moral or religious principles

Continentals: Regular armed forces

convoy: Group of ships traveling together for safety

court martial: To try him before a military court for offenses against military law

crow's nest: A shelter or platform fixed near the top of the mast of a vessel as a place for a lookout to stand

decoy: Imitating a turkey call to lure a turkey toward the hunter's position

deferment: Postponement from the draft

devastating: Highly destructive

dismount: Get off their horses

dispatches: Messages

disrupted: Destroyed or interrupted

draft card: A card sent by the federal government telling someone they must enlist in the military, often done in wartime

endeavored: To try hard to achieve something

exemplary: Outstanding

faced about: To turn and face in the opposite direction

flamethrowers: A weapon that sprays out flaming fuel

fledgling: Inexperienced, brand new

flogged: Punishment with a whip or a stick

foxholes: A hole in the ground used by troops for shelter

French Huguenots: French Protestants

frigate: A sailing ship with one gun deck

gamecock: Feather of a rooster bred and trained in game fighting

garrisons: Permanent military installations

golden chance: An excellent chance to accomplish a goal

grapeshot: Ammunition consisting of small iron balls fired together from a cannon

grappling hooks: Device with iron claws attached to a rope in order to tie up to another ship or dock

grenades: Small bombs thrown by hand

harass: To make small scale attacks on the enemy

Hessians: German troops hired by the British to help fight against the Americans

homespun: Simple homemade clothes

honeycombed: Filled with cavities or tunnels

imminent: Sure and about to occur

impressment: Forced to serve in the military

incessant: Something repeated without pause

inciting: Causing or instigating

indigo: A tropical plant of the pea family, which was formerly widely cultivated as a source of dark blue dye

intimidated: Frightened into changing one's mind or plans

just: Morally justifiable

K.P.: Kitchen patrol

kamerad: Used by German soldiers in World War I as a cry of surrender

kamikaze: Desperate military maneuver

left flank: Side, generally a weaker spot

Lindsey-woolsey: A strong coarse fabric of linen and wool

loon: A large black and white bird with red eyes

maneuvered: Skillfully arranged in a strategic position to gain an advantage

midshipman: Naval cadet

militia: A military force raised from the civil population to be called up on short notice

Muslims: Followers of Islam

mutinous: Sailor who is willfully disobedient and causes trouble

muzzle flashes: Light from the sudden release of a firearm

nohow: In no way

objector: A person who for reasons of conscience objects to complying with a particular requirement, especially serving in the armed forces

outposts: A detachment of troops stationed at a distance from a main force to guard against surprise attacks

palmetto: A type of palm tree

partisan: Member of a fighting force that fights in secret

partisans: Strong supporters of the cause, fighting secretly

pay dirt: Struck its target

pennant: Flag flown from the masthead

picket lines: Small units of soldiers watching for an enemy advance so they can warn others

America's War Heroes

pickets: Soldiers posted on guard ahead of the main force

pillboxes: Concrete dug-in guard posts with holes from which to fire a gun

pounds: British money

powder monkeys: Boys employed on a sailing warship to carry powder to the guns

private: Lowest rank of enlisted personnel

privateers: Armed ships owned and operated by private individuals authorized for use in war by the government

procuring: Acquiring

quarter: Mercy

Quasi-War: An undeclared naval war fought from 1798–1800 between the United States and the French First Republic or "Pirate Wars"

quench: Put out, extinguish

ransom: Release of a prisoner in exchange for a sum of money or another captive

regiment: A military unit consisting of up to 10 companies

rifleman: An infantry soldier armed with a long-rifled gun

rigging: Masts, cables, chains, and ropes that hold up the sails

right smart: A great deal

routing: Defeating and causing to retreat in disorder

satchel: An explosive on a board lifted with a rope

scheming: Plotting, planning

sciatica: Pain affecting the back, hip, and outside of the leg

scoffed: Mocked

scoundrel: A dishonest person

secession: To leave a political union

sharpshooters: Elite corps of riflemen who provided precision shooting

skirmish line: A preliminary battle involving troops in front of the main force

squadron: A group of warships

stalking: To pursue stealthily

strategically: In a way that relates to a military advantage

tactics: Strategies, plans

Tora! Tora! Tora!: Literally means "tiger" in Japanese, but implied a lightning attack

Tory: Colonists who supported Britain

tourniquets: Tight bandages to stop major blood flow

traitor: One who betrays his country

treacherous: Involving betrayal

trench foot: A painful condition of the foot caused by long exposure to water or mud

Tripolitans: Persons from Tripoli

Uncle Sam: Term meaning the United States government

upland: Hilly ground above sea level

vanished: Disappeared

veterans: Men who had fighting experience

volley: When an attacking army lets loose a barrage of bullets all at once

wagoner: A person who drove a wagonload of supplies across the mountains

Yankee: Northern sympathizers

Yanks: A broad term in World War I to refer to all Americans

America's War Heroes

Corresponding Curriculum

The *What a Character! Series* can be used alongside other Master Books curriculum for reading practice or to dive deeper into topics that are of special interest to students.

This book in the series features American war heroes, whose stories would incorporate well for students in grades 6-8 accompanying history, language arts, vocabulary words and definitions, as well as geography studies and cultural insights. We have provided this list below to help match this book with related Master Books curriculum.

Chapter 1: Ethan Allen and His Green Mountain Boys

America's Story Vol. 1

The Fight for Freedom

America's Struggle to Become a Nation

Language Lessons for a Living Education

Chapter 2: Daniel Morgan and His Sharpshooters

America's Story Vol. 1

The Fight for Freedom

America's Struggle to Become a Nation

Language Lessons for a Living Education

Chapter 3: Francis Marion, The Swamp Fox

America's Story Vol. 1

The Fight for Freedom

America's Struggle to Become a Nation

Language Lessons for a Living Education

Chapter 4: John Paul Jones, "I Have Not Yet Begun to Fight"

America's Story Vol. 1

The Fight for Freedom

America's Struggle to Become a Nation

Language Lessons for a Living Education

World History

World Geography and Cultures

Chapter 5: Stephen Decatur and the Pirates

America's Story Vol. 2

Language Lessons for a Living Education

World History

World Geography and Cultures

Chapter 6: David Farragut — Boy at Sea

America's Story Vol. 2

Language Lessons for a Living Education

World History

World Geography and Cultures

Chapter 7: John Mosby — The Gray Ghost of the Confederacy

America's Story Vol. 2

Language Lessons for a Living Education

Chapter 8: Sergeant York — Unlikely Hero

America's Story Vol. 3

Language Lessons for a Living Education

World History

World Geography and Cultures

Chapter 9: Jake DeShazer — From Prisoner to Preacher

America's Story Vol. 3

Language Lessons for a Living Education

World History

World Geography and Cultures

Chapter 10: Desmond Doss — The Unarmed Hero

America's Story Vol. 3

Language Lessons for a Living Education

World History

World Geography and Cultures

Endnotes

1. "Ethan Allen Captures Fort Ticonderoga, 1775," EyeWitness to History, www.eyewitnesstohistory.com (2010).

2. Ethan Allen, *A Narrative of Col. Ethan Allen's Captivity in History in the First Person: Eyewitnesses of Great Events: They Saw It Happen,* ed. Louis Leo Snyder and Richard B. Morris (Harrisburg, Pa.: Stackpole Co., 1951), Original Sources, accessed January 12, 2023, http://www.originalsources.com/Document.aspx?DocID=LFQELMCMI4STL9W.

3. Albert Blaisdell & Francis Ball, *Hero Stories from American History* (Boston, MA: Ginn and Company, 1903) 113.

4. Ibid, 114.

5. Homer Colby, *Mace's Beginners History* (New York: Rand McNally and Co., 1909) 186.

6. Blaisdell & Ball, *Hero Stories from American History*, 117.

7. Ibid., 117.

8. Ibid., 118.

9. Lawton Evans, *America First — One Hundred Stories from Our Own History* (Springfield, MA: Milton Bradley Company, 1929).

10. William Mace, *A Beginner's History* (New York: Rand McNally and Co., 1921) 190–191.

11. Mace, *A Beginner's History*, 192.

12. Gardner Allen, *A Naval History of the American Revolution, Vol. II* (Boston, MA: Houghton Mifflin Company, 1913).

13. Dwight J. Zimmerman, *"Lt. Stephen Decatur, Jr. Burns the Philadelphia,"* DefenseMediaNetwork, October 31, 2014. (https://www.defensemedianetwork.com/stories/lt-stephen-decatur-jr-burns-the-philadelphia/).

14. Mabel B. Beebe, *Four American Naval Heroes* (Project Gutenberg EBook, 2011) 137, gutenberg.org

15. Ibid., 144.

16. Loyall Farragut, *The Life of David Farragut* (New York: D. Appleton, 1891).

17. John S. Mosby, *Mosby's Memoirs: The Memoirs of Colonel John Singleton Mosby* (New York: Barnes & Noble Digital Library, 2012), 108.

18. Ibid., 109.

19. John Munson, *Memoirs of a Mosby Guerrilla* (New York: Moffat, Yard and Company, 1906), 46; also Jonathan Daniels, *Mosby: Gray Ghost of the Confederacy* (New York: J.B. Lippincott, 1959), 63–64.

20. All quotations from *Alvin York, Sergeant York: His Own Life Story and War Diary* (Garden City, NY: Doubleday, Doran and Company, Inc., 1928).

21. C. Hoyt Watson, *The Amazing Story of Jake DeShazer* (Winona Lake, IN: The Light and Life Press, 1956).

22. Frances M. Doss, *Desmond Doss — Conscientious Objector: The Story of an Unlikely Hero* (Nampa, ID: Pacific Press, 2005), p.102.

A CLASSIC PRESENTATION OF GOD'S REDEMPTIVE PLAN FOR MANKIND

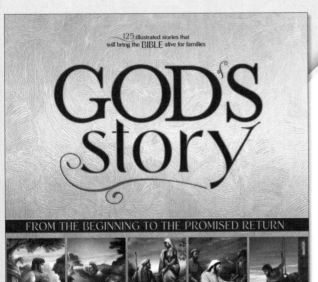

978-1-68344-288-2

This beautifully illustrated book of Bible stories will delight both children and adults! Enjoy short, easy-to-read examples of God's transforming power in the lives of biblical believers and skeptics. Revisit the moments that reveal God's love for us — from the Fall in the Garden of Eden, to the judgement of the Flood, the trials and triumphs of Israel, and the promise of a Savior, through doubt, rebellion, and despair, these events lead us to the gift of Christ among us and the promise of eternity with God.

spreads from the book

Master Books®
A Division of New Leaf Publishing Group
www.masterbooks.com

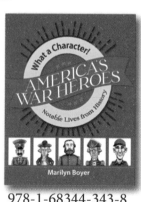